# DETACHED ATTACHMENT

THE ESSENCE OF TRUE HAPPINESS

KRISHNA GANESH

**Woven Words Publishers OPC Pvt. Ltd.**

**Registered Office:**

Raipur, P.O: Raipur Paschimbar,

Dist: Purba Midnapore, Pin: 721401,

West Bengal, India.

**Branch Office(Operational)**: H. No. 8-1-346/19/A/1 & 2, Flat no. 504,

5th Floor, Zara Residency, Brindavan Colony

Toli Chowki, Hyderabad 500 008, Telangana.

www.wovenwordspublishers.com

Email: publish@wovenwordspublishers.com

First published by Woven Words Publishers OPC Pvt. Ltd., 2018

Copyright© Krishna Ganesh, 2018

NON-FICTION

IMPRINT: WOVEN WORDS NONFICTION

ISBN 13: 978-93-86897-33-6

ISBN 10: 9386897334

Price: $35/₹500

The author asserts the moral right to be identified as the author of this work.

All rights reserved. This book is sold to the condition that it shall not, by way of trade or otherwise, be lent, resold, hired out, or otherwise circulated without the publisher's prior consent in any form of binding or cover other than that in which it is published and without a similar condition, including this condition, being imposed on the subsequent purchaser.

Printed and bound in India

*I dedicate this book to my father Sri. Raghupathy Acharya and my mother Smt. Sukanya Raghupathy whose support, love and blessings have moulded me into what I am today. Also, through this book, I want to express my heartfelt gratitude to my brother Sri. Santhosh Kumar and his wife Dr. Chetana, my sister Smt. Roopa and her husband Sri. Shivaprakash. They all have been the pillars of support for us during our testing times.*

# Table of Content

Acknowledgement
**Preface**
- Introduction to the book
- Why is this book written?
- Clarifications about this book

**Bhagavat Geetha – Karma Yoga**
- What makes BG so special?
- Circumstances that led to the revelation of BG
- Arjuna's anxiety
- What is Varnashrama?
- What is Varna Sankalana?

**Krishna's consolation**
- Krishna's recitation of BG
- Reality of life
- Human body is aging, so it is changing every moment
- Choose work according your Varna
- Life has a purpose
- Duryodhana will never let you live peacefully
- Perform every action with a sense of detachment
- Absolute surrender to the divine brings detachment in life

**Analysis of detached attachment**
- What is attachment?
- Problem with attachment
    - Craving for recognition

- - Attachment to work
  - Over-indulgence about image
- Over-attachment to everything one perceives to posses
- Over-attachment to material objects
- Over-attachment to people
- Other hardships attachment brings to the fore
- What is detachment?
  - Detached man during bad times
  - Detached man during good times
  - How a detached man treats his work?
- Other advantage of being detached in life
- How to develop detachment in life?
- Do everyone develop detachment during difficult times?
- Contemplation and questioning are the pre-requisites for detachment
- What's next?

**Universe**
- The vast expansive Universe
- The mighty solar system
- The vivacious nature Earth and her beauty
- Everything in the Universe is interconnected
- Krishna has the answer to what drives the functional Universe
  - Brief introduction to Brahman as per Scriptures
  - Body cells perform intelligent tasks
  - Who made the cells intelligent?
  - What is this force called?

**Universe is made up of only energies**
- Introduction
  - Universal creation

- Universal dissolution
- Five differences which persist until eternity
  - Difference between Aatmas
  - Difference between material objects
  - Difference between Aatma and matter
  - Difference between Aatma and Brahman
  - Difference between matter and Brahman
- Every Universal activity is performed by various energies
- Living species as per Padma Purana – a 5000 year Scripture

## Aatmas and their Gradation
- What is Kaksha for an Aatma?
- List of Aatmas on various Kakshas

## Divine Aatmas
- Macro level
- Micro level
- Divine energies
  - Chaturmukha brahma
  - Vishnu
  - Rudra
  - Mukhya Prana
    - Pancha Pranas
    - Pancha upa-Pranas
- Other Aatmas behind the Micro and Macro level activities
- Do human Aatmas have gradation?
- Man is influenced by divine and evil energies
- Shimshumara – the center of the Universe
- Dhruva Nakshtra – North star
- The Universe has directions

**Asuric Aatmas - Evil energies**
- Introduction
- Nature of Aatma
- Gradation of Asuric Aatmas
- Battle between Asuras and Devas
- Mahabharata – the war of worlds
- Do humans have the ability to influence others?

**Universal energies control humans**
- Energies have Gunas
- Our sensory organs drive our mind
- Food we eat has direct bearing on our mind
- Food has Gunas too
  - Sathvik food
  - Rajasik food
  - Tamasik food
- Effects of nature induced forces on humans
- Aatmas have inherent Gunas
- Energies have colors
- Aatma being energy has color too

**Intelligent forces behind every Universal activity**
- Demigod Chandra is behind the functioning of Moon
- Macro world
  - The deity of Vanaspathi
  - The deity of Anna
- Micro world
  - Seeing
- Demigod Vivasvan is behind the functioning of Sun

- Macro world
  - Season formation
  - Water evaporation
  - Cloud formation
  - Photosynthesis
- Micro world
  - Seeing
- Human body and Pancha koshas
  - Annamaya Kosha-AK
  - Pranamaya Kosha-PK
  - Manomaya Kosha-MK
  - Vijnanamaya Kosha-VK
  - Anandamaya Kosha-AK
- Tripurushas and the Pancha Koshas
  - Shareera Purusha -SP
  - Chanda Purusha -CP
  - Veda Purusha -VP
- Conscious memory - CM
- Subconscious memory -SCM
  - Our beliefs stay in SCM
  - Deep knowledge on any subject stays in our SCM
  - Our deep desires find its place in the SCM
- Pranamaya Kosha – the brief introduction
  - We breathe 21,600 times an hour
  - Inner calendar is different
  - How to delay aging?
- Brahman is responsible for everything
- Pranas in the micro world
  - Pancha Pranas
  - Pancha Upa-Pranas

- Pranas in the macro world
- Sensory Organs and their deities
- Manas is everything
- Functions of Manas
- Science behind our communication
- Complexity of speech in a nutshell
- Thoughts are complicated too

## Everything depends on Brahman for existence
- Is Brahman that indispensible to the Universe?
- Man is in one of the three states
    - Sleeping
    - Dreaming:
    - Waking
- Other activities humans involuntarily perform
    - Seeing
    - Eating
    - Breathing
    - Working
- Why demigods have to depend on Brahman?
- How powerful is Brahman?
- Definition of "Bhagawan"- the most revered title for GOD

## Subtle moves the gross
- Subtle mind moves the gross body
- What does Vedanta say about the doership?
    - Vishwa Chakshus
    - Vishwa Karnah
    - Mahashanh
    - Vishwa Shilpih

- The sound byte of every language is the epithet of Brahman
- Is Brahman responsible for the intelligence in the demigods?

**Karma Theory in a nutshell**
- Karma theory in brief
- Concept of Sthitha Prajna (SP)
    - A strong purpose in life is essential for becoming SP
    - Leading a detached life can lead us to the state of SP
    - Example to illustrate Sthitha Prajna from Mahabharata Epic
    - Only an SP can become a true Karma Yogi

**Nishkaama Karma – an analysis**
- Nishkama Karma (NK) in brief
    - Complexities involved in bringing NK to life
        - Expectation
        - Why our efforts often do not fetch anticipated returns?
        - Develop the sense of equanimity
    - How to develop the feeling of non-doership all the time?
        - The concept of object and its mirror image:
        - Aatma has no wherewithal to perform any activity
        - If someone makes apple pie, what is his Aatma's involvement in it?
        - Why Aatma feels that he does everything?
- How work really happens?
    - What happens if we identify ourselves as the real doers?
    - What should be our attitude when we perform any action?
- We get what we deserve not what we desire
    - How is this linked to Nishkaama Karma (NK)?
    - How to practically apply this concept at work?

## Everything is predestined
- Is everything predestined?
  - Universe is in the tight grip of divine
    - Infinitely complex mathematics is behind the creation
    - Solar system – complex machinery at work
    - Lets delve more into it with local examples
    - Life is a puppetry
- Logical analysis of controlled human life
  - Everything is stage-managed
  - Who creates the environment for everyone?
  - How does the divine make us take wrong steps in life?
- Divine creates environment for controlling everything
- Does the "philosophy of predestination" encourage idleness?

## The purpose of life
- Does life have any purpose?
- Karmas
  - Sanchita Karma
  - Prarabda Karma
  - Aagami Karma
- Is divine grace required to bring a sense of DA in life?
- Do all Aatmas attain Moksha?
  - Nature of Aatma
  - The Guna of an Aatma
- Number of births is pre-destined
- Pain OR pleasure we enjoy in life is to erase Karmic impressions
- The divine tightly controls the evolution of an Aatma through various births
  - Shrusti
  - Sthithi

- Laya
    - Jnana
    - Ajnana
    - Bandha
    - Muktha
    - Moksha
- Should we stop doing our regular work and instead pursue GOD?
- How to gain spiritual knowledge?

## Intellectual and intuitional flashes

- Introduction to Observation and Contemplation
    - What is Observation?
    - Why we rarely observe things?
- The pitfalls of not cultivating the art of observation
    - Diseases are not detected at the early stage
- What is contemplation?
    - Deep thinking is a part of contemplation
- Intellectual VS intuitional flash
    - How to get IF?
- Past examples of Intuitions
    - Archimedes
    - Sir Isaac Newton

## Knowledge and bliss are within us

- What is bliss?

## Conclusion

# Acknowledgments

I humbly prostrate to Sri Ananda Theertha – an incarnation of Sri Mukhya Prana - Anjaneya, who is the greatest among all Aatmas, whom I consider as my eternal Guru. His constant remembrance has facilitated the spiritual awakening in me. Also, I modestly bow down to my beloved Lord, Sri Krishna – a Universal GOD, for equipping me with everything required for writing this book.

I dedicate this book to my father Sri. Raghupathy Acharya and my mother Smt. Sukanya Raghupathy whose support, love and blessings have moulded me into what I am today.

I would like to thank my beloved wife Veena for all her assistance in writing this book and special thanks to her for proofreading the manuscript. I thank my brother-in-law, Prasad Tantry and his wife Ramya Tantry for their support and best wishes.

I sincerely thank my sister Roopa and her husband Mr. Shivaprakash Chandra, my brother Mr. Santhosh Kumar Raghupathy and his wife Dr. Chetana for all of their encouragement over the years. They have been pillars of support for me especially when I lost my two and a half years old beloved child Srinidhi in 2008.

I would also like to thank my Guru, Shri. Bannanje Govindacharya for teaching me the art of soul searching in life. His advice to do serious introspection on the God, nature and my life has got me answers for some of the most difficult questions about life. The revelation came out of my contemplation later became an inspiration for writing this book.

Last but not the least, I thank all the wonderful souls who have directly or indirectly helped me in writing this book.

# Introduction to the book

From the time immemorial, man's quest has always been to find ways to be happy in life. All his actions from dawn to dusk reflect that. He does every work in pursuit of happiness. However, happiness is one thing that is elusive of him, as it is not got easily. Philosophers of the yore contemplated on it and came out with the view that man can only be blissful in life when he realizes that he is a part of the "whole Universe".

Living with the sense, "I am a part of the Universe that is protected by the divine" brings the feeling of physical and emotional security, which are prerequisite for happiness. If not, his feeling of insecurity will keep him on the edge and rip him apart due to the fear of the unknown, which is the mother of all sufferings. There is truth in what the Philosophers concluded about happiness. They said GOD is the real caretaker of the whole Universe, in which man is also a part. So, naturally, he is also being taken care of.

They added, everything - from the smallest microbes, which are at the lowest end of evolution, to the human beings, which are at the highest end of evolution, live under the constant divine protection. They seek power from the divine for their very existence.

One observation to note is, every other living being on the planet lives blissfully, except the human being. Upon close examination as to why he is not blissful, what comes to the fore is his "false ego". He got this "false ego" because he is blessed with an intellect by the divine, which other living beings do not have. The intellect gives him the arrogance, which is the byproduct of his ego. The arrogance comes when he is intoxicated with power OR money OR both. The more he is intoxicated, the less submissive he becomes and more egoistic he gets.

This is how the gift from the divine soon turned out to be a curse from the divine to him. He started using his gifted intellect to do evil things – being deceitful to the society for selfish gains.

As a result, he is mentally disconnected from the Universe and proudly feels independent - not a part of the Universe, which is safeguarded by the divine. The consequence of it is misery - fear, anxiety, depression, and others. Nevertheless, the moment he understands that he is very much a part of the Universe, all his pain and distress will melt away and he becomes fearless.

Now the question is, how to experience that in life? – Vedanta (Holy scriptures) suggest that the man's only purpose of living should be to realize GOD. To do that he has to make all his day-to-day activities revolve around GOD and that's when he gets enlightened. The enlightenment brings the realization that everything in the Universe is under the constant divine protection and he can live carefree without any fear.

Again, one more question arises now, How to realize GOD? - Vedanta recommends daily worship of GOD through elaborate rituals to seek divine grace, which is of foremost importance for GOD-realization.

Man trod this path to attain enlightenment and eventual liberation for over several millennia as the world remained mostly spiritual back then. However, with the time, the world too started changing slowly towards more and more materialism and dharma – righteousness, took a back seat. People started feeling empty OR hollowness inside. The world slowly lost the divine consciousness and as a direct result, people started leading adharmic life – the life of vices. The erosion of dharma was so much that kingship got into the hands of the evil rulers, who brought much pain and sufferings to their innocent citizens.

To set everything right, the divine took the incarnation of Lord Krishna (LK) some 5000 years ago. LK explained Arjuna – one of the Pandavas while reciting Bhagavad Geetha at the threshold of "Mahabharata war" – an epic war, how to perform every action in life. The Lord proclaims all actions be performed with the sense of "Nishkaama Karma" (NK) – action without any expectations, as a service to GOD. NK will eventually invoke the required divine grace for GOD-realization. In fact, one must treat every action as a divine duty and perform it with a sense of service to the Lord, with truthfulness and sincerity. That's when work becomes worship to the individual and it will elevate his consciousness towards the divine. When work becomes worship, man doesn't have to worship GOD separately to invoke HIS grace, his day-to-day work itself can do that. Lord Krishna showed to Arjuna, how a war can be a worshipful act when it is done as a duty in the service of the divine. LK also talks very high about a state called Sthitha Prajna (SP) - a mental state of equanimity. He claims that only those who have become SP OR achieved that state mentally can only perform every action in the way of NK.

**Why is this book written?**

A lot has been said about NK over a long period of time through books and lectures and yet the confusion remains. The reason is, there is no proper approach (roadmap) towards NK, as people (mostly laymen) find it difficult to understand and incorporate it into their lives.

I have tried to practically explain in this book the way to get the sense of NK through a concept called detached attachment (DA) that one should first cultivate in life.

When one cultivates and practices DA in life, he gets transformed into an SP eventually. Only an SP who has achieved the mental state of equanimity can grasp the true essence of NK and perform every action in that way.

In a nutshell, DA is the foundation for becoming SP to perform every activity in the form of NK, which is a must for GOD-realization. Pictorially it can be represented as follows.

DA ————> SP —————>NK————->GOD realization

However, getting the sense of DA is the toughest nut to crack in life. Somehow man tends to gets attached to everything he lays his hands on. Attachment comes out of wrong knowledge, which is the byproduct of ego. DA can kick in when one seriously observes his and others' lives, the society he lives in, nature, the animal kingdom so on and so forth.

The following eternal truth pop out of the observation

Temporariness of everything in life - Nothing is permanent in life, everything has to end one day.

Non-doership of anything in life - No one does anything in life, only divine does.

Everything is fore-ordained in life - No free-will, everything is pre-destined in life.

The feeling of detachment sets in when anyone starts pondering on the above subject. Still for a deeper and wider sense of detachment, one should philosophically understand the "Universal law of nature"- the eternal truth behind everything that governs the

Universe. Through this book, I tried to rationally explain the truth in a layman's language.

## Complexity of explaining the philosophy in a simple common man's language

Though I have a deep interest and some understanding of philosophy, I wasn't sure as to how a serious subject like philosophy can be explained in the layman's language. Despite the difficulties, if I have written the book, it is the courtesy of the divine which guided and directed me through intuition as to what I have to write, where to start and where to end. I humbly give the honour to the divine for making me write this book. So, the credit should go only to the divine, not me.

I am heavily influenced by the philosophy of the 11th-century saint Madhvacharya (1238 AD ~ 1317 AD), who advocated the philosophy of "Tatwavada". So, my writing will reflect it profusely.

More information about the saint can be got here.

https://archive.org/details/Philosophy.of.Sri.Madhvacarya

## Clarifications about the book:

I want to clarify that this book is written not to promote any religion OR to preach ethical living to the readers. Hence, it is not-at-all a religious book.

The intention behind writing this book is to explain the concept of "detached attachment (DA)" – a mental state, which can truly bring lifelong happiness. In fact, it is an honest attempt to explain the concept of DA rationally so that everyone can easily understand and benefit from it. If one is able to crack DA in life, he will be able to execute every action with the sense of NK, which will eventually lead to the attainment of Moksha (loosely translated as liberation in English). The detached attachment is nothing to do with the following

- Breaking up the ties with family & friends and walking away.
- Relinquishing the responsibilities and becoming a recluse.
- Lazing around.

The detached attachment is everything to do with the following

- Understanding the limits of everything we come in contact with, in our day-to-day life – men, material, and events, and live life accordingly.
- Everything in life is fore ordained, so lead a life of contentment and joy.
- Understanding the fact that nobody does anything, it is the divine does it through us based on our past Karmas.
- We always get what we deserve not what we desire and everything happens for a reason.
- Developing good relationships with people.

- Bringing spiritual and material excellence in life, yet have a lot of humility.
- Becoming a true lover of the divine.
- Attaining Liberation (Moksha in Sanskrit) after escaping from the jaws of birth & death.

What detachment can do the least is, put a full stop to unnecessary thinking and worrying about the future. A man who is detached in life, will not worry about his OR anyone's future as he is well aware that "what is not destined, won't happen, do what may ". At the same time "what is destined, will happen, do what may to stop it". So, he knows that his "worrying" OR "not worrying" will do nothing to alter the divine plan as he has zero control over it. He will do to the best of his ability, whatever he can do and leave the rest to the divine. This way he will lead a happy and carefree life.

**Gautama Buddha (480 BCE ~ 400 BCE)** preached his students to cultivate the inner stillness OR calmness to achieve lasting happiness in life. His view is, if one doesn't develop inner stillness, one often gets internally disturbed (ID) for various reasons. The internal disturbance doesn't let anyone be at peace with himself and in that case, he can't be at peace with others as well. The root cause of all - hatred, strife and violence in the world is because of this.

When one is internally disturbed, he cannot perform any action correctly, let alone being happy. All his works will be of substandard quality because he can't concentrate on his work. So, as per Buddha, one should strive to achieve inner calmness at all cost. To achieve inner stillness, one has to develop DA in life. When one is attached to everything one perceives to be in possession, he can never be at peace in life so the inner calmness eludes him permanently. Developing the sense of DA should be the first priority for him.

Also, I have touched upon the controversial topic "fate and free will" to know if we have any freedom to shape and drive our lives. The philosophy of the divine is a difficult subject to digest. Unless we understand it, we can't get hold of NK, which is very important for the early completion of our "perpetual" journey towards the infinite and attain Moksha (liberation). Everything in the Universe, which deserves Moksha, is on a perpetual journey towards the infinity and the scriptures say HE (abode of GOD) is the final resting place for all of them.

I have touched upon "Karma Yoga" of BG that LK speaks about. With this, now, let's begin our philosophical journey by deep diving into the other chapters.

## Bhagavad Geetha – Karma Yoga

### What is Bhagavad Geetha?

Bhagavad Geetha (BG) is a 700 verses treatise narrated by Lord Krishna about the philosophy of life and its purpose, which became the foundation for spirituality for the mankind. The sage Vyasa - one of the incarnations of Lord Narayana himself, authored BG, a part of the great epic "Mahabharata", over 5000 years ago. In fact, he classified, segregated and wrote the ancient scriptures like "Vedas, Puranas, Mahabharata, Upanishads" etc. for the mankind to preserve for the future and study them. Prior to that, from the time immemorial these scriptures were being learned and taught orally, as per the tradition back then.

### What makes BG so special?

It is the quintessential of Vedanta, as it touches all the subjects of philosophy and encapsulates the essence of the entire Vedanta itself. That makes it "the panacea" for all kinds of problems one faces in life and also aids in the upliftment of consciousness from the levels of the animal to human to divine. That means, it (BG) has the ability to bring GOD consciousness in the ordinary man.

Also, the BG attains significance because of the place and the circumstance under which it was narrated. The place was Kurukshetra – a land where 2 huge armies were just waiting to slaughter each other and the circumstance – just a few moments before the war actually broke off on the ground. The place and circumstances signify "our lives at the crossroads" and BG - the nectar from the Lord, signifies the "divine force" that can bail us out of turbulence.

Circumstances that led to the revelation of BG

The circumstances which led to the narration of BG by the Lord are very interesting. Just before the epic Mahabharata war broke out, huge armies of Pandavas and Kauravas assembled at Kurukshetra facing each other. That's when Duryodhana, the crown prince of Indraprastha glances his army and the army of his enemy. Suddenly, he develops fear when he sees the enemy soldiers all around the horizon just waiting for the orders to kill him and his army. Even though he had some of the best warriors of the time siding him and his army being bigger than his enemy's, he still feels his army is weak and he thinks it is due to the absence of the war-hardened warriors. The gripping fear psychosis and lack of self-confidence make him believe that he would lose the war, which he eventually did after 18 days into the war.

That's when his minister for defence – Bheeshma Acharya gives a green signal to his army for getting ready to start the war by blowing his conch; by then, from the side of Pandavas, Krishna blows his conch. Other Pandavas also blow their respective conches signalling their army to get ready for the war. By the time war was about to start, Arjuna asks his charioteer Lord Krishna to bring the chariot just in between the 2 armies to see who all have assembled to get killed by him. His pride/ arrogance and overconfidence makes him say so. When Krishna brings the chariot to space in between the 2 armies facing each other, Arjuna started developing cold feet after seeing his own kith and kin, with whom he grew up waiting to die. For him, they seem to be waiting on the enemy side to be butchered away. His beloved great-grandfather Bheeshma Acharya and his gurus - Dhrona Acharya and Kripa Acharya, who taught him archery and made him what he ultimately became known to be, were all on the enemy side.

## **Arjuna's anxiety**

Arjuna, out of grief makes the following statement to Krishna *"Dear Krishna, what a bad day for me to see my own relatives and friends standing on the opposite side and I have to fight and kill them to win this war, what? - For a mere kingdom? Also, whom should I celebrate the victory with? When the entire grief-stricken country will be mourning the death of her nearest and dearest, where will our enthusiasm for celebration be? In fact, we will* become responsible for all their miseries and will have to burn in hell until eternity as a punishment for our evil deeds."

He is making the statement out of attachment and wrong notion that he is the doer of everything. Krishna says nothing and keeps his smile on his face as usual. Then Arjuna continues, "*Krishna if the kingdom is what is at stake if I do not fight, it is OK with me to let go. Instead of enjoying the kingship of the kingdom that will be earned by killing millions of people, I would rather let Duryodhana keep our share of the kingdom too and prevent massive bloodshed. Rather, I would preferably go to a forest and meditate than fight like animals for trivial things. Like everyone, we too have to die one day. Tell me, Krishna, will we take anything from here when we depart from this life? –NO, we only take the outcome of good or bad deeds we do, here on earth. Then, why wage war and kill millions of innocent soldiers who have no gains - economical or spiritual whatsoever, fighting this war?*"

Arjuna gets too emotional and feels weak out of confusion, as his future seems to be appearing hazy for him. Then again he adds "*Krishna when all the adult men, who have assembled here to fight, die in the war, only teenage boys OR old aged men will remain in the kingdom. By then every adult woman would have lost her husband and become a widow in the kingdom. Any society without adult men will lead to chaos, as there would be no man to ensure the security of women.*

*Also, these women in their adulthood may digress out of bodily need and may end up with unethical pregnancies, which will result in Varna Sankalana*".*

Arjuna feels so weak to even sit firmly on the chariot; his mind is full of doubts. With parched tongue and trembling arms and mind full of confusion, he throws up his weapons on the ground, gets on to his knees and begs Krishna with folded hands, *"My dear Krishna, you have been my savior, a guide, and a friend. Kindly tell me what I have to do now, I am getting so restless that I may collapse here itself. Please show me the way."*

Krishna now decides to help Arjuna by giving following BG narration, as guidance to him. He never tries to intervene when Arjuna was blabbering his frustrations onto Krishna. He (Krishna) never moved by Arjuna's emotional outbursts, rather kept his cool and listened to every word of Arjuna with patience. Krishna broke his silence only when Arjuna requested him with folded hands to help him out.

By this, he showed to the world that one should never give unasked advice to others, as it would mean nothing to them.

Before getting into Krishna's exclusive reply to Arjuna's dilemma, let's understand the meaning of Varna Sankalana, which Arjuna has used in his statement and to know that we should first know the meaning of "Varnashrama*". What is Varnashrama?

Varna is the classification of humans based on the profession they do, not the caste OR class into which they are born. If we look at any society, we find 4 types of people.

(a) Those who are thinkers and they constitute 2% to 5% of the population of any country. They have interest in the knowledge and ability to do research and development (R&D) - Brahmins

(b) Those for whom leadership, administration, protection comes naturally - Kshatriyas

(c) Those for whom business, finance, economics are their natural flavor - Vysyas

(d) Those who do not have any of the above 3 qualities, but they are good in providing service to all the above three Varnas - Shudras.

These skills are natural, as they are there in every human being at the genetic level, and are called Varnas - Brahmin, Kshatriya, Vysya, and Shudra. However, every individual has a mix of all the Varnas and whatever is dominant, he belongs to that Varna.

So, during the Vedic times, that is very long ago, maybe over 10,000 years ago and beyond, people used to choose professions based on their Varna - their inherent abilities to do any job. So, they used to marry within their Varna only, to produce progeny belonging to the same Varna for building strong societies.

The children so produced could become really good Brahmins, who could meditate, contemplate/ analyze and discover various aspects of nature like Astronomy, Astrology, Medicinal science, Material science, Nutrition, Mathematics, GOD etc.

Similarly, children so produced could really become good Kshatriyas who had the natural affinity towards administration and were courageous enough to protect their societies from enemy invasions.

Also, children born out of wedlock of Vysya couple attained world class in agricultural production and economy due to their inbuilt abilities, which was good for society.

Shudras born from Shudra Varna would be inherently helpful to the society, as the above three Varnas needed people to assist them. This is called Varnashrama.

### What is Varna Sankalana?

People earlier feared that if intermixing of Varnas happened, the character OR nature of the baby born out of such wedlock might not adhere to the true Varnashrama system.

That means, it would result in social disorder, an intellect-less Brahmin doing the knowledge-based work, a courage-less and incapable person ruling a kingdom as a king, etc.

Their intention was not to disturb the Varnashrama system, which was there since time immemorial. They strongly believed that disturbing Varnashrama would create a weak and moral-less society. Any society is deemed to be weak and unfit to live when people take up professions not based on their inherent abilities OR Varnas.

For example, a Brahmin doing Vysya's work, a Kshatriya doing Shudra's work, a Vysya getting into the garb of a king and a Shudra wearing the hat of a Brahmin.

This is because the progeny born out of such wedlock lacks inherent abilities to do their jobs. Due to this, they face professional failures creating chaos everywhere. Such a society is dangerous and unfit to live. This is called Varna Sankalana, which Arjuna was insisting in his argument.

## Krishna's consolation

### Krishna's recitation of BG

Krishna gave a big smile to Arjuna and said, *"Wake up Arjuna, first of all, you should not forget that you are a warrior and a knowledgeable person. I am surprised that you made all these childish rants that too at an inappropriate time, which do not suit your stature"*. Arjuna gets flabbergasted and gets even more confused, as he feels difficult to digest the allegations put forward by Krishna, that his statements are childish.

### Reality of life

Krishna continues, *"Arjuna, what makes you think that these people (friends, relatives and others) will die in the war because of you? First of all, you come out of the illusion that you are going to kill these people. For your information, no universal power can ever kill anyone if his end hasn't come. Also, no power can save anyone, if his end has come. For your information, it's the divine power that does the killing OR saving, using various instruments and that's the eternal truth.*

*These people are here because their lives have reached "the end" stage. So I, in the form of Mruthyu (Death in English) have to annihilate them, to bring an end to their lives. In this process you are just an instrument (like a sword) in the hands of Mruthyu (me) to kill them, that's all. Like no weapon has the power to either kill OR save anyone on its own, you too have no power to either kill OR save anyone on your own. Remember, everywhere I call the shots and I have decided to kill these people using you. So, that's going to happen whether you like it OR not, and no power in the Universe can ever change OR stop that".*

Krishna pauses for a while and Arjuna takes a deep breath, as he is unable to digest what he heard. He is amazed and fearful at the same time by the startling revelation made by Lord Krishna.

Krishna resumes, "*Arjuna, you should know, whoever is born has to die one day and that is the law of nature. Moreover, the death is to the body, not to the indwelling Aatma. The body will age after living for several years and one day it will collapse and get trashed. Aatma, on the other hand, will get liberated from the aged/ worn out body and gets an opportunity to enter into a new body, which is younger and healthier. This is exactly like someone changing his soiled, torn clothes with new/ fresh ones. Clothes may get trashed, not the wearer.*

*These people, who are at the threshold of war, will also lose their bodies and their Aatmas will move into new bodies, as the process* of being born again. Therefore the cycle of birth & death is endless".

## Human body ages, so it is changing every moment

Arjuna interjects now by asking, "*Krishna, I have not seen the Aatmas of people with whom I grew up, but I identify them with their bodies. After their body is gone, they are gone forever and that's my concern. It doesn't matter to me if the Aatmas are permanent or not, as their Aatmas aren't visible to my naked eyes anyway. So, once I lose their bodies, I lose them permanently.*"

Krishna replies beautifully to this question, "*Arjuna if you are concerned about losing their bodies, then you have to worry about that on a daily basis. This is because the physical body changes every moment due to the process of ageing. So, whatever body you see today, is not the same tomorrow and whatever body you see tomorrow, it's not the same the day after, since the body changed again, as it has aged by one more day.*

*Arjuna, you should understand the eternal truth – a newly born baby grows into a child, a teenager, an adult, an old person and finally embraces death in a matter of a predestined timeframe due to internal changes. These changes constantly happen inside the body every moment, non-stop. So, there is absolutely no point in worrying about things which you don't have control over.*"

Arjuna still not convinced about why he should not renounce the ill-fated war, go away to the forest and lead the life of a hermit. Krishna nudges him and continues.

### Choose work according to your Varna.

"*Listen Arjuna, you wanted to run away to a forest and meditate the rest of your life, right? - This is "the stupidest idea I have ever heard so far. It doesn't bind to any of the rules of Varnashrama. You know, everyone has to do his duty based on the Varna he belongs to. You are a Kshatriya, so your duty should be to administer, give protection to your subjects, and fight for the upholding of righteousness OR dharma in the society. So, your duty currently is to do whatever required protecting dharma, if that involves killing your own kith and kin, so be it.*

*In fact, even imperfectly done work belonging to one's own Varna will fetch far better returns than perfectly done work belonging to some other Varna; it is that serious.*"

Krishna makes this very clear to Arjuna; even then, he (Arjuna) thinks Krishna is not addressing the issue he raised, like Varna Sankalana and after-effects of killing own kith & kin.

### Life has a purpose

Krishna adds to what he said earlier "*Also there is a purpose behind every life, what better way to make it worthwhile than fighting for a cause? Tell me Arjuna. In your case, it is to uphold dharma. Very few people in this world will get this kind of once-in-a-lifetime opportunity. So, even if you die fighting for this cause, you will reach heavens and enjoy the fruits of your good work there. If you win the war, you will anyway enjoy the fruits of your success here in this mortal world.*

## Duryodhana will never let you live peacefully

*Moreover, even if you want to relinquish everything and go away to a forest to lead a life of a recluse, Duryodhana won't let you do that, as you are an existential threat to him. He will never let you live peacefully there, as he perceives you to be his enemy number one and will make every attempt to kill you. So even if you don't want the war now, you will end up fighting him later. Fighting is inevitable and not a choice for you. So, right now fight like a professional warrior, with full of courage for the cause of upholding dharma."*

Arjuna interrupts again saying "*Krishna, with the massive bloodshed and destruction resulting due to the war, won't I be held guilty for spilling the blood of innocent people? Won't I attract bad Karma as a consequence of my bad actions? Is it not sin to kill people? Krishna, please help me clarify this.*"

## **Perform every action with the sense of detachment**

Krishna compassionately puts his hand on Arjuna's shoulder and says, "*Listen Arjuna, there is nothing called good action OR bad action in this world. Any action is just an action, whether it is good OR bad is depending on the intentions behind it. So, when an action is done with good intentions, it will fetch good returns. Similarly, when done with bad intentions, it will fetch bad returns. Here your intentions to fight and kill the opponents is to uphold dharma, which is for the societal good. You are not going to kill anyone for your selfish gains and that's the difference. To put it in simple terms - if there is a selfish motive behind any work, even feeding the hungry people can fetch bad Karma. On the contrary, if the motive is to help others OR doing good for the society, then even killing can attract good Karma.*

*When someone does his work selflessly like this, he is said to be doing his work detachedly. In fact, one should perform every action with "absolute detachment" without any expectations, but as a service to GOD with full devotion, that's when it becomes "Yajna" - (sacrifice in English).*

*So when one's action becomes Yajna, one can see GOD in every work he does and that's the essence of Karma Yoga*".

## **Absolute surrender to the divine brings detachment in life**

Arjuna gets a doubt about detachment and he asks, "*Krishna, how to do any action selflessly?*" - For this Krishna replies, "*The selflessness can only come with self-surrender to the divine. However, the self-surrender can come when you have a profound love for the divine.*

*This deep-rooted divine love (Bhakti in Sanskrit) can only come from the divine knowledge (knowledge about GOD) itself. So, the more one knows about GOD and his qualities, the more he loves HIM. As a result, more he will surrender to the Almighty. This is like a vicious circle, each feeding onto the other*".

In a nutshell, Krishna indicates that if one tries to perform any action without divine love (Bhakti) and divine knowledge (Jnana), one can never perform the action with the sense of detachment. He (the doer) invariably does it with lots of attachment and that is the prelude to his downfall in life. In fact, the root cause of all the human miseries is the sense of attachment to everything one does and everything one seems to possess.

So Krishna's ultimate message to the mankind is, for happiness and Moksha, one should lead a life that looks to be "attached" at the outset but in reality, "detached" from the inside. This is called as "detached attachment". Let's analyze the "detached attachment" statement in detail.

# Analysis of Detached Attachment

Krishna wants everyone to perform every action selflessly as a service to GOD. When we do our work that way, a sense of disengagement sets in. That is the secret of a happy life and the way towards liberation (Moksha in Sanskrit).

Why Krishna talks highly about detachment? Let us first understand attachment and detachment separately.

### What is Attachment?

Man has the intellect to think and make decisions based on situations. He has a mind to express his feelings through emotions and this is why & how he is different from an insentient object like a rock or a stone. Now through the same mind, he develops strong feelings like "I", "me", "myself", "mine", "what's in it for me?", etc., all the time. He gets these feelings around anything to everything he comes in contact with. This is called an attachment. In fact, his struggle in life is around them only. These feelings are also called as his "ego".

All his sufferings – pain, anxiety, sadness, stress, insomnia, anger, arrogance, low self-esteem and many more, arise out of attachments.

## Problems with attachment

### Craving for recognition:

Man generally seeks recognition from the society he lives in and more so from his peers and superiors in his office. The feeling is driven by the sense of "I" makes him restless and gives him an enormous amount of anxiety. If he doesn't get the expected recognition in the office, his mind will never let him rest peacefully, since all he wants is, the recognition by "hook or crook". Therefore, he indulges in getting it somehow. In doing so, he wastes all his valuable time politicking, gossiping-about-others, playing gimmicks, etc. What he doesn't understand is, there is no shortcut for the "coveted recognition" anywhere, be it inside the corporate world or outside. It is not earned easily; one has to work hard towards achieving it.

His craving for recognition by any means will blind him from this truth and makes him take wrong decisions in life. The result is, he can't be at peace and suffers from anxiety, depression, etc. This comes out of the attachment towards "Me".

## Attachment to work

Also, when someone is driven by a huge sense of attachment to his work, he can never take any criticism sportingly - be it about himself or his work. If someone says something negative about his work, he is unable to take it objectively; rather he would take it personally and spoil the relationship. He feels people are out there to humiliate him. His legs and hands tremble out of anger, heart starts beating fast and breathing becomes shallow. What follows next is the emotional outburst and heated arguments, thus bringing an end to his personal development. He does behave like this because he suffers from "low self-esteem" and for him, any criticism about his work means that people are trying to degrade him by finding fault in his work.

This is also resulting out of attachment towards "Myself".

## Over-indulgence about good image

People generally have expectations when they visit any social gatherings that they should be profusely greeted like important people. They feel let down and not cared for in case they perceive any shortcomings in the way they are greeted. For them, what people think about them, their image matters a lot than anything else. Again, this happens due to excessive attachment towards "Me".

## Over-attachment to everything one possesses

Man generally gets "over" attached to his possessions and suffers because of that. Let's see how it affects him

Over-attachment to material objects

It is natural for a man to get attached to his belongings – vehicles, property, money, Jewellery, etc. However, there is a hitch in doing that as he will never be at peace after all. For example, if he is over-attached to his car, he gets too worried if there is a scratch or a dent on the car, formed accidentally either by himself or by others. He will never get sleep and is concerned till his dent or scratch is removed, whatever may be the cost. This overindulgence in keeping his things intact will never let him be happy in life. He should know the limits of these objects and learn to live with imperfections. If necessary, he should let go of this at times to be contented and happy in life. This is also applicable to all his other material possessions.

Over-attachment to people

Man tends to be a control-freak if he is overly attached to his family and friends. He gets into the act of advising them on what they should or shouldn't do, all the time. This way he is unknowingly trying to control others, which will always bring him pain. People will never behave as per his expectations and hence he will have to live with the pain throughout his life unless he detaches himself from his people.

## Other hardships which attachment brings to the fore

A man who leads a life of attachment, cannot bear with even the smallest of problems in life. He gets too emotional and when the conditions in life deteriorate even a bit, suicidal thoughts constantly start running in the back of his mind. Such people suffer from the following:

- Lack of courage and being highly emotional
- Uncontrollable anger
- Nature of seeking revenge
- Being impatient all the time
- Feeling restless over unimportant matters
- Being highly argumentative and quarrelsome over trivial matters
- Bloated ego and its repercussions.

Therefore, too much attachment brings only sorrows in life and that's when living may seem to be a liability for the person.

Now, what if he loses the above-listed feelings? – The result is detachment.

## What is Detachment?

The moment someone hears this word, he gets confused with renouncement and living in solitude. But that's not the case in reality. Detachment means knowing the limits of everything a man comes into contact with – events, people and objects and leading life accordingly.

## Detached man during bad times:

A man who is detached will lead a normal life exactly like others. He too will face vagaries of life – moments of happiness and sadness like everyone else. However, the difference is, he won't get influenced by them (events). When he is passing through a bad patch in life, he will do whatever required to turn the tide against him. In case he fails in this endeavour and the outcome is not encouraging, he is not disheartened as he has the satisfaction that he tried his best.

He knows that there is a higher power, which he cannot overpower it. He understands pretty well that this higher power or the divine power has the final say over everything in the universe, including his life.

Since the divine has brought the bad time due to the fruits of the past bad Karmas, he accepts the divine verdict wholeheartedly and adapts his life accordingly. He understands that there is no way one can go against the storm. He will patiently wait for his good times to roll in and do whatever he can with the knowledge that everything has to change one day, including his bad times.

## Detached man in good times

During his good time, he is neither overly elated nor he is brazenly exuberant. He is aware that the higher power, which has the final say over everything, has blessed him with happiness and is humble enough to accept that. He never lets his success get into his head and is always grateful to the divine.

He believes that his good time is the result of his good Karma of the past. To reap good things in his next life, he continues to do good work in the present life, as he knows the eternal truth that man reaps what he sows.

So naturally, he is more cautious and never flaunts his richness. He is modest and humble while interacting with people.

## How a detached man treats his work?

A detached person, be it a film director, an office manager, a research scientist, an entrepreneur, a father or anyone for that matter, will not have "My" attached to his work. He considers every work - from the household chores to mundane office works; any work that benefits the society to the one that benefits himself and his family, as "GOD's work" and does it with full dedication, devotion, integrity, and sincerity.

His focus is only on the professional execution of the work, that is, to meet its objectives. It is not so for earning a good name and fame (N&F). He is well aware that "one will always get what one deserves, not necessarily what one desires". So, if he deserves N&F, he will surely get it, if not, no hard feelings at all for him.

This is because he treats both success and failure with equanimity, so no "Hoo-ha" whatsoever, either over the success or failure of his work. He enthusiastically takes full responsibility for his work and stays truly duty bound.

Following are the benefits of working without "My" attached to the work:

- It's easier to get into the clients' shoes and evaluate the work.
- Work can be easily dissected without any hard emotions to find the lapses when there is one.
- Criticism about work can be taken objectively without the feeling of despair.
- It is effortless to own up work failures without feeling "shameful" and "loss of face".
- If required it's easy to take the blame and shield the team from criticism. Never pay any attention to silly/ senseless matters, so no arguments.

- Will have the magnanimity to let the team take credits if the end-result is a success.

He may experience failures or victories in life but is not-at-all influenced by them because he has achieved a state of no-turmoil from inside - a rare feat.

## Other advantages of being detached in life

There are many more advantages in being detached in life -
- Life gets as joyful and blissful as it could.
- Detachment makes life happier, brings-in sense of humor.
- Relationship with everyone improves.
- Life will be purpose driven and always duty bound.
- Integrity, truthfulness, honesty, and humility get intertwined in the genes.
- Good character boosts a good reputation in the society.
- Never lazes around and indulges in cheap gossips.
- Anger will be the thing of the past.
- No anger means no grudge or revenge-taking attitude.
- A state of equanimity sets in.
- Equanimity leads to inner stillness during good and bad times.

## How to develop detachment in life?

It is very difficult to say what triggers the sense of detachment in life. The cause, however, varies from person to person.

Generally, when a man goes through difficult times in life, his journey towards detachment starts. But one shouldn't confuse depression with detachment. People get the feeling of superficial detachment when there is a death in their house or when their businesses fail or when they go through a family crisis like divorces, etc. The point to note is, depression also looks like detachment. However, the difference is, the feeling of "hopelessness" and "anxiety" drives it. Also, depression is dangerous and suicidal so the patient has to take psychiatric treatment at the earliest.

The true detachment starts when a man is passing through difficult times and he begins to observe things, as they are and commences self-questioning like "Why things are like this?" "Where did I err?", etc.

In fact, more the difficulty he is in, high is the likelihood of him getting the sense of detachment in life. During the bad patch of his life, he will understand the philosophy behind detachment much better, that too on his own. He does that by seriously observing everything he comes in contact with, in day-to-day life. By going to the bottom, he will experience a lot of things previously unknown to him. This will lead him to know the limits of what he can do and what he can't do, what is in his control and what is out of his control. Knowing that will fetch him the answers he is seeking from life. The answers will, in turn, make him come to terms with life, which results in contentment. A contented life will ultimately trigger happiness.

## Do everyone develop detachment during their bad times?

Absolutely Not! The reason is people don't contemplate deep enough about life. The moment bad times hit him, he begins his blame game, blaming everyone but himself for the downfall. His energy and focus are only around that since his mind is fully disturbed due to anxiety, depression, and rage. With this kind of mindset, he will never be able to do meaningful contemplation, which is a pre-requisite for detachment.

So the result is that hardly anyone contemplates intensely for detachment to set-in. With 99.9% of people being like this, we can conveniently say, none will get detachment in life.

Contemplation and questioning are pre-requisites for detachment

Man has to contemplate seriously in life, to understand why things are the way they are. Serious contemplation happens only when the chips are down in his life and it (deep thinking) will lead to many things, previously unknown to him. The questions like "Why is my life this way? "Why do I deserve this?", will lead to Karmas – past, and present. From there, it will get into understanding the nuances of Karma and its effects. From there into some something else next and the list goes on and on.

As he progresses in his quest for truth, he slowly becomes aware of the temporary nature of life. He realizes that many forces are at play, which have a direct influence on his life. Also for him, life itself looks more like a drama, which is scripted and directed by the divine force and has NO control over it. People come to his life at the right time, play their roles and go away. Everything is temporary and has to end one day. Death is the inevitable end of life and no one can escape from its jaws.

Also, he gets to know that no one, absolutely no one takes anything when he departs from life. The name, fame, money, property, etc., behind which people put their "sweat" and "blood" suddenly appear meaningless to him as they only boost his "false ego", that's all. That's because none of these are permanent in life and they rather create more harm to him than good.

Now, he understands clearly that when he dies, he carries with him nothing other than the fruits of good and bad actions he performed. Thinking about and doing good for others becomes important to him than anything else from now on. When he experiences this truth even a bit, detachment starts kicking in. However, the detachment can be shallow and superficial if the contemplation is not deep enough.

Lord Krishna in Bhagavad Geeta* states, *"Arjuna, when someone seriously contemplates on any subject, he will find me at the deepest level"*. Upanishad states, *"Tena vina truna mapi chalati"* – Not even a straw of grass moves unless GOD wishes so. That means the entire Universe is in the tight control of GOD and hence things happen only as per the desire of the divine. HE is the pure essence or the backbone of everything and the ultimate power behind all the Universal activities – right from the subatomic level to the cosmic level. So, HE makes things happen and hence he is the doer of everything. Ultimately, it is HIS grace that brings the detachment in one's life.

## **What's next?**

The sense of "attachment" should always accompany the sense of "detachment". This is because man has to live in the material world and do his duties as a disciplined soldier without any expectations. He cannot run away from his responsibilities by putting his family and friends in deep trouble. In fact, the society has given that right only to ascetics. They can stay fully detached from everything – men and material and remain attached to GOD alone. However, they shouldn't have their own personal family; rather everyone in the world belongs to their family.

Also, Lord Krishna doesn't endorse detachment alone in the BG for the mankind. Instead, HE wants man to develop the sense of "detached attachment" in the place of detachment alone. Lord explains it through the following verses in BG in the 5th chapter,

"*brahmaṇy ādhāya karmāṇi*

*saṅgaṃ tyaktvā karoti yaḥ*

*lipyate na sa pāpena padma-patram ivāmbhasā*"

One who does all his works detachedly by dedicating them only to Brahman, that is ME, then all the sins arisen out of his works will not stain him like the water can never wet the leaf of the lotus plant. The lotus plant grows only in ponds, as it needs water to stay alive. However, no matter how much one tries to wet its leaves, they remain dry as the water drops off as droplets from the leaves. Nothing sticks to its leaves, not even the dust.

Lord Krishna recommends this to mankind. He says that man has to lead his life like the way a lotus plant lives in the water. Although the plant remains in the water, its leaves are always clean. The plant remains dry and clean, as water cannot wet it. So, to say the least, man has to continue living in the material world amidst his family, relatives, and friends but not get affected by any of them.

Man with this kind of mindset appears attached to everything from the outside, but the truth is, he is completely detached from the inside. His heart is full of love and carries no enmity or grudge against anyone, so he is very happy. This kind of mindset is termed "Detached Attachment".

To understand and perform every action through the way of "Nishkama Karma (NK)", one should develop the mindset of DA first. For that to happen, one should have the clarity on the doership - who is the real doer? - "Me" or "someone". To get a clear picture on the doership, one should understand the 3 entities properly

- God,
- Aatma - oneself,
- Nature

and their interplay. I have tried to explain these 3 entities by touching upon "Karma Yoga" by Bhagavad Geeta*. It is important to understand various energies at play in the Universe and how they influence and drive us to perform actions. However, they (intelligent energies) too are not independent to do things on their own, something else drives them too. One should understand this "doer" who drives even the demi-gods (intelligent beings) do things, is THE real doer. Who is he? – Brahman OR Narayana.

The concept of DA looks too idealistic. Is it accomplishable? – Yes, provided we understand properly the concept of non-doership. We are not the doer of anything in life, rather some divine power does everything through us. In fact, the essence of everything we see, do, eat, meet, interact, etc., in our lives is divine. As per Vedanta, it is experiencing this "hard to digest" truth – one that can liberate us from all our bonding and attachments. Finding the true doer of everything should be the motto in life.

Krishna gives a clue about it in BG by stating, *"Arjuna, I decide as to who has to rise and who has to fall in life"*, *"Who has to be pampered and who has to be damned in life"*, *"Who has to live and who has to die."* *"I create the environment for all of these to happen based on the individual's past karmas"*, *"I call the shots everywhere"*.

That being the case, it is the divine grace that is far more important to get the feeling of detached attachment, as it is the first step towards Moksha (liberation). Nonetheless, contemplating on the truth by understanding the philosophy behind it, hastens the pace of detachment. Let's look into the Nature to understand this philosophy.

Detached Attachment| *Krishna Ganesh*

# Universe

**The vast expansive Universe**

The Universe with billions of galaxies, stars, planets, asteroids, interstellar gas objects, dark matter, etc. looks astonishing to everyone. The Milky Way is a massive barred-spiral galaxy, which contains our solar system and the astronomers estimate that over 100 billion stars are present in it. The diameter of the Milky Way could be 100,000 to 200,000 light years. To approximate its length, we must first know that the light travels at a speed of 299,792 kilometers per second. From this, we can find out how far it will travel in one minute, one hour, one day, one week, one month, one year, 100 years and finally 200,000 years. It is impossible to express such a huge number through words and that is the length of the diameter of our Milky Way, which is not even a speck in the Universe when we see it in entirety.

However, in the Milky Way, every moment stars are born and then they die. Once born, they live for the period they are supposed to and they die. The surprising point to note is, the stars take several thousand light years to take birth, live for millions of light years and their death also takes thousands of light years. However, all these numbers vary from star to star. The Universe is driven by activities every moment.

It's thrilling to look into the sky in the night as it can inspire hoards of thinkers and philosophers into creative thinking. The some of the stars are so far from the earth that their light reaches us million or sometimes billion years later. There is the dark matter – (roughly 80 percent of the mass of the universe is made up of material that scientists cannot directly observe) and black holes – (When the stars die they shrink to become ultra-dense objects called black holes), which make the Universe highly mysterious to everyone.

So, to our finite mind with a limited grasping power, everything seems to be in disarray. However, the reality is quite the opposite - everything is in absolute cohesion with each other. They are created that way and operate with the clock- precision efficiency. Since the functioning of the Universe is very orderly and with an iron- grip kind of control over it, nothing can go wrong, ever. Also, the Universe appears to be due to material cause only but in reality, there is a spiritual cause behind it. That means, there is "a spiritual reason" behind why the Universe is what it is today. The spiritual reason is to enable the consciousness of the Aatmas (loosely translated as souls) to evolve from the animal level to human to the divine level and finally enter the kingdom of GOD and live there for eternity.

What kind of spiritual force is behind the making of the Universe? – To realize the truth, let us look at our solar system for some clues.

## **The mighty solar system**

When we see our solar system, we see the planets revolving around the gigantic sun on their dedicated tracks with utmost discipline.

Every planet takes a pre-determined period to complete each revolution. Everything is happening with clock precision. Nothing can ever go wrong because one planet going off the track means colliding with the other. This will wreck the equilibrium of the entire solar system. Since nothing happens on its own, there is something that is making the solar system work with absolute precision. What is that? – Let's look into nature for the answer.

The Vivacious Nature Earth and her Beauty

When looking into our planet, we see nature, which aids the regular seasonal changes, the beautiful flowers, chirpy birds, mountains, oceans, seasonal fruits, shrubs, large trees, waning and waxing moon, etc., that's sufficient to turn even an ordinary person into a poet.

Nature in all her glory looks like a beautifully dressed up young bride and can even be compared to a mother, as she gives shelter to and nurtures every living organism on the planet. When we observe nature, we get the feeling that there is some force behind the working of nature, which makes her behave the way she is behaving. <u>What force is that?</u> – an infinitely intelligent being.

## **Everything in the Universe is interconnected**

In the cosmos, every object has an influence on every other object as they are eternally connected with each other. That means, any event happening in one cosmic object will have a direct OR indirect impact on the others. The events like the death OR birth of a star, the union OR separation of galaxies, the movement of cosmic bodies from one place to another, so on and so forth have an influence on the other. However, the time taken to influence depends on the distance of these bodies from the place where the events occurred. For example, if any star that is 5000 light years away from the earth dies today, its effect on the earth is felt after 5000 years from now. The monsoon pattern may get affected by the past cosmic events, which may have a bearing on monsoons per say.

So the Universe needs to be understood as a whole, not in bits and pieces. This is what the modern astronomy is talking about nowadays.

Likewise, human life also is connected with many things – the food we eat, the work we do, the friends we hang around with, the office environment, the boss we report to, the client we provide services to, etc. They all have a profound influence on us. Let's understand the interconnection in brief

For example 1:

If someone is complaining of a headache, it may be due to indigestion he is suffering from. Indigestion may be due to disturbed or shallow sleep. That may be due to anxiety and stress. Anxiety may be due to excessive work in the office and a demanding boss as others are dumping their work on him. This may be because he is unable to say "NO" to the work dump. That may be because he lacks the self-confidence. Finally, the root cause of his ailment appears to be the lack of self-confidence. So, his treatment will be "paracetamol" tablets for temporary relief from a headache and "counselling" for a permanent cure of a headache.

This is how the symptoms and their causes come out when we contemplate deeply. It is true of every issue we face in life. We can resolve it only by going to the bottom of it through deep thinking OR soul searching.

Example. 2

If someone is suffering from a lack of quality sleep, he could do deep dive right into his sleeplessness by asking questions, "Why do I get disturbed sleep?" "Am I anxious & worried while going to bed?" "If so, how to keep my worries away while sleeping?" so on and so forth. If he contemplates on sleep, he will surely get an answer to the following questions "What exactly is sleeping?" "Is it rest to the mind OR body?" "If it is to the body, then despite lying in bed for nearly 6 hours, why am I not feeling rested?" "If it is to the mind, I lay in bed for nearly 6 hours yet I do not feel fresh, why?" That's when he will realize that sleeping means giving rest to the mind. Throughout the day, the mind is active with one thought or more. Giving rest to the mind through sleep is the real gift to mankind. When someone sleeps like a log, none of his worries, pain and health issues bother him. The moment he is awakened from deep sleep, all his pain, worries, etc. come back to haunt him. The truth is when in deep sleep, there is absolutely no thought in the mind and it is empty. Except for the awareness of the "self", nothing is inside it. So, the mind seems to be at deep rest. The outcome of a good night's sleep is joy and happiness. So, it is the mind which brings pleasure or pain to man. The mind gets its feed in the form of thoughts supplied by various sensory organs – eyes, nose, skin, tongue, and ears. In a way through the mind, man experiences his pain or pleasure. However, if the mind is kept busy by engaging it with something or the other, one can be happy. That "something" can be any thought that brings joy to him. In case the mind is kept blank without any thoughts, even then one can experience bliss. Only when the mind is full of worries or negative emotions, it may end up bringing fear, anxiety, and sadness to the individual, which will result in diseases. However, while lying on the bed to sleep, the mind needs to be empty without any thought to get good sleep. So, the empty mind is the key to a good night OR restful sleep. The philosophers of the yore, who were on the lookout for ways to be happy in life, got inspired by sleep. Their view was, "while sleeping, if the empty mind is what brings rest and joy to humans, why not keep the mind empty even in the waking state?" That led to the "Zen meditation", which teaches how to be meditative throughout the day, by keeping the mind empty of thoughts, yet have laser focus/concentration on the work one is doing.

This is how a simple contemplation of sleep to know the reason behind a headache, led to the mastery of the mind. It is that amazing. This shows how everything in the Universe is connected to every other thing and the connection is eternal. Using this connection, our mind can attract anything from the Universe if we seriously desire and it is known as "mind power".

For example:
If we desire deeply for rains and we being in that thought consistently, then it results in heavy rains when and where we want. The mind has the ability to do whatever required including the pulling of the water-bearing clouds from elsewhere to bring

rains when and where we want. This is so because our thoughts generated in our minds are energies. The desire gives rise to thoughts in the mind, which in turn strengthens our desire. The strong thoughts bring a strong desire to us and vice versa. Deeper the desire, more powerful is our thought and more potent it gets to get us what we want in life. This is the power of the mind and the strength of our desire. It is not a fiction; it can very much happen in our life. So, it is important that we have desires in life but only positive ones, which can give us the feeling of accomplishment.

Now, there is one infinitely intelligent and powerful energy that connects everything in the Universe and makes it function the way it should. <u>Who is this? What kind of energy is it?</u>

## Krishna has the answer to what drives the functional Universe

Lord Krishna says the Universe is actively governed by various divine powers or divine energies. They perform every activity – from the micro level to the macro level across the Universe, under the direct supervision of an infinitely powerful energy. Krishna claims that HE is that power.

While explaining Bhagavad Geeta to Arjuna, Krishna talks about the Universe in chapter 15. He quotes the Universe is made up of three fundamental entities, "The individual Aatmas (loosely translated as souls), the matter and the supreme Aatma. Every Aatma in its purest form is energy.

He classifies the individual Aatmas into two categories:

**Kshara Purusha (KP)** - All living Aatmas possessing material and perishable bodies, subject to the cycle of birth and death, are called KPs.

- Gender of Aatma: – Aatmas have gender and unique identity. There are masculine and feminine Aatmas with eternal names.
- Gunas of Aatma: - Every Aatma under KP category has its own Guna - loosely translated as the quality of its inbuilt nature. The nature of an Aatma can be compared to the nature of a seed, for example, a grape seed will yield grapefruits, a mulberry seed will yield mulberry fruits and an apple seed will yield apple fruits. This exclusivity comes from the Guna of that seed, which is its inherent quality. Hence it can "never-ever" change, no matter what is done to change it.

Likewise, Aatmas too have their own qualities brought out by Gunas and they are forever permanent. Gunas, in turn, are classified into 3.

- Sathvik – These Aatmas are GOD loving and support the divine law of nature.
- Tamasik – These Aatmas are GOD hating and oppose the divine law of nature.
- Rajasik - These Aatmas are neither GOD lovers nor GOD haters; they are self-centric and love themselves the most.

**Akshara Purusha (AP)** - The AP is one Aatma, which is feminine in nature and is ever free from the cycle of birth and death, which has an imperishable body made of pure energy, which is the force behind the entire material universe. Matter, in the words of Krishna, is all the non-living entities like mud, rock, metal, ore, etc.

**Purushottama** – The one Aatma, which is infinitely superior to both KP & AP and is masculine in nature, is called Purushottama or the Supreme GOD (Brahman in Sanskrit). Purushottama, in reality, is beyond any "gender". The Brahman is the inner dweller of everything (perishable and non-perishable) and makes every activity (from micro to macro levels) happen.

The entire creation, sustenance, and destruction of the Universe happen because of HIM. In fact, Brahman is the source of all spiritual and material worlds and everything emanates from HIM and dissolves into HIM. For the individual Aatmas, Brahman is the giver of intelligence, knowledge, freedom-from-doubt and delusion, forgiveness, truthfulness, control of the senses, control of the mind, happiness and distress, birth, death, fear, fearlessness, non-violence, equanimity, satisfaction, austerity, charity, fame, and infamy.

## A brief introduction to Brahman as per scriptures

Our body is directly under control by some force. "Manduka Upanishad" states that the 3 states of man, which are "sleeping", "dreaming" and "waking", are because of this force. Any given time, we are in one of the above states with the help of that force. It is the same force that carries out all actions, which happen within our body during these states.

Also, we all know that our bodies are made up of tissues, organs (liver, kidneys, heart, lungs, stomach, etc.), bones, bone marrows, blood, so on and so forth. Each of these is made up of cells which in turn has atoms filled with electrons, neutrons, etc. Since each organ is made up of cells, it is the individual and the collective working of these cells which make the organs function to secrete hormones.

To our dismay, all these body parts including the cells are insentient and none can work on their own.

## Body cells perform intelligent tasks

The cells intelligently pick and absorb what is required for their organs to function. For example cells of the liver will pick only those nutrients from the bloodstream that are required for the liver to function. Similarly, the cells of the kidneys pick nutrients from the bloodstream, which are required for the kidneys to function. Likewise, the cells of all the organs of the body absorb nutrients required for their respective organs to function. Also, they eject cellular waste into the blood from where it is removed from the body as excreta.

## Who made these un-intelligent cells intelligent?

The same universal force that makes the heart beat and makes the lungs pump fresh oxygen to billions of cells and carry carbon dioxide from them to the outside. The same force makes the complex communications in humans happen by converting the thoughts, which arose in the human mind into verbal communication by twisting the tongue in various fashions, combined with lip movements. It is really astonishing to know that the time taken for the thoughts, so arisen, until their deliverance through a language, from the mouth is in microseconds. So, unless this is well planned and organized, communication can never happen this easily.

Similarly, the act of seeing in us happens because of this force. It identifies the images of the objects that fall on our mind through our eyes. It conveys the meaning of the same to our intellect and ultimately to us. Through emotions, we get to know about what we are seeing and it happens in Nanoseconds. To put things in perspective, each and every action (from simple to complex) within our bodies happens because of this force.

Also, if we see nature, we can see the seasons (spring, summer, monsoon, winter), living beings - animals, birds, insects, worms, etc. living in rivers, seas, mountains, forests, so on and so forth, live harmoniously. They are all well fed and their needs are taken care of. The phenomena like sunrise and sunset, earth's revolution around the sun and rotation on its own axis happen with clock precision. Since they are all insentient, they require an intelligent force to make things happen.

**What is this force called?**

It is Brahman OR fondly known as Lord Narayana or GOD. As per "Upanishads", Brahman is limitless and has infinite qualities. HE is all-pervading, infinitely powerful and the knower of everything. The same scriptures claim that HE is the force behind each and every action that takes place within the universe and outside. The actions – be it creation and destruction of the Universe, movement of giant astral bodies like stars, galaxies, etc., birth and death of galaxies, constellations, illumination of stars to the movement of the minutest particles like electrons in the atoms are all performed by this force or Brahman, the infinitely knowledgeable. Brahman uses many demigods to execute all the activities happening within and outside the Universe.

# The universe is made up of only energies

## Introduction

Everything in the Universe – the individual Aatmas, the matter and the Brahman, is pure energy in the primordial state.

The Aatmas, electricity, gravitation, magnetism, buoyancy, thunderbolt, various atmospheric forces (lift, drag, thrust & weight), etc. are energies. Similarly, sunlight (VIBGYOR– various shades of light), light from the thunderbolt and light from the fire are energies too. Added to them, the 5 elements which man experiences in his daily life, that is Earth, Air, Fire, Water & Ether are also energies in their primordial state.

So, the matter is nothing but energy in its ionic state. The base material, which forms the entire material universe including organic matter – gross bodies of all living beings encompassing plants, shrubs, and trees, is the same.

## Universal creation

During the universal creation, the ions group together to form various atoms. Every atom has subatomic particles – negatively charged electrons and the core dense space called the nucleus. The nucleus contains positively charged protons and neutrons - which have no charge and are spinning inside it. On the contrary, electrons orbit the nucleus.

The number of protons in the nucleus determines what kind of element an atom is. To explain briefly – oxygen atom has 8 protons spinning in the nucleus. The presence of 8 protons makes the atom, an oxygen element. Similarly, 7 protons inside the nucleus of an atom make that atom a nitrogen element. When the number of protons inside the nucleus of an atom is 9, then the element is fluorine when it is 10, it is neon, when it is 79, it is gold. silver has 47, iron has 26 protons, etc., in their respective nuclei and the list goes on.

This is how the material Universe is built with just the arrangement of subatomic particles in the atoms.

## Universal dissolution

The entire material Universe is broken into pieces and each piece is further broken into the ionic state. So the material universe will come back to ionic form as a result of Universal dissolution. It will remain so until the Universal creation starts after a long gap and this cycle of creation-dissolution activity goes on and into eternity.

## The five eternal differences

These following differences exist always and let's look into them

## Difference between Aatmas

We have seen that every individual is unique and it is true even between children born out of the same mother's womb and the same father. What makes them unique? – Is it the body? – NO, there can be some similarity between siblings like in twins as far as looks are concerned, that's all. Then? – It is the uniqueness of the Aatmas, which contributes to the uniqueness of the individuals. This will persist forever.

## Difference between material objects:

Every object is different from every other object and this difference remains so until eternity. For example - No two leaves of the same tree or of different trees are exactly 100% the same, though they look similar to our naked eyes. But under the microscope, they are totally different. Similarly, no 2 fruits of the same tree or of different trees taste exactly the same. There is a subtle difference, which our tongue cannot distinguish. However, when examined in the laboratory for their constituents, the difference can be detected using advanced lab equipment.

## Difference between Aatma and matter

Though both are pure energies in their primordial state, Aatmas are sentient beings, meaning they have consciousness with mind and intellect, so they can think and make decisions. Matter lacks these and remains un-intelligent hence insentient in nature. So, every matter is different from every Aatma. Both can never be even similar, let alone being the same.

## Difference between Aatma and Brahman

No Aatma can ever be compared with Ishwara, be it on any of the exclusive qualities that the latter possesses. Ishwara's potencies are of infinite scale – Universe and beyond. There is absolutely no match between them. This will remain so until eternity.

## Difference between matter and Brahman

Matter can never be compared with Ishwara as the difference between them remains infinite. So, they remain different forever.

All these differences make sense only when nature OR the material Universe is real, not illusions as some philosophies claim. This eternal truth of 5 differences was first put forward by the 12th-century saint Madhvacharya, which gives the spin to the Vedanta.

## Every Universal activity is performed by various energies.

Nothing in the Universe, absolutely nothing happens on its own as a coincidence or as an accident. If something has happened, there is always a reason and a doer behind it. If a raw orange has ripened, there is some power that has turned the orange ripe. How can a sour/ bitter tasting raw orange turn into a sweet juicy fruit, when it ripens? – Someone is at work behind it. It's just that we never thought about it. Even if we want to understand, our very limited intellect cannot grasp this Universal truth.

When we extend the same principle, we can see every activity in the universe – from the spinning of electrons around the neutrons in an atom to the blooming of flowers in a plant, the molecular activities inside every living creature to the galactic movements in the outer space, all these are happening because of the Universal energies. That means numerous energies are involved in performing these activities in the Universe.

Since matter is inanimate and has no intelligence, it can't execute these activities on its own. Something else is involved. So, what could that be? – The individual Aatmas - the only other entity left. A few of these Aatmas, grouped under Kshara Purusha, are super intelligent energies having Universal scale potencies. They execute all the Universal activities with clock precision as envisaged by the divine. The Universe what we see today is because of them. These Aatmas are divine and the rest form 8.4 million different living species, as per Bhagavad Geeta. The human being is one of the 8.4 million species and the most evolved than the others.

The truth is, even these divine Aatmas, which seem to be responsible for performing all the activities of the material Universe, are not performing on their own. Another infinitely intelligent being called Brahman or Purushottama or GOD does them (actions) through the divine Aatmas. Brahman uses the divine Aatmas as instruments to perform every activity, so naturally, HE (Brahman) is the real doer of everything. HE alone has the infinite freedom; power and the knowledge to perform activities and the rest are all dummies. This sticks to the universal principle "Always subtle moves the gross" (let us understand this concept later).

For an un-intelligent common man's eyes, it appears as though he himself (self) is performing the actions and this is where the entire problem lies. This misguided knowledge leads to the notion of the "I" –the ego, which is the root cause of all the evils.

## Let's look into the break down of various species of life.

Species as per Padma Purana – a 5000 years old text

Another ancient Hindu text "Padma Purana" which is also as contemporary as Bhagavad Geeta not only says that there are 8.4 million different species on Earth but also goes a step ahead and categorizes or classifies them as follows:

- Jalaja (Water-based life forms) – 0.9 million
- Sthavara (Immobile living beings - plants and trees) – 2.0 million
- Krimayo (Reptiles) – 1.1 million
- Pakshinam (Birds) – 1.0 million
- Pashvah (Terrestrial animals) – 3.0 million
- Manavah (Human-like animals) – 0.4 million

8.4 million life forms in all! Now, let us try to understand the concept - gradation of Aatmas.

## Aatmas and their gradation

**What is Kaksha for an Aatma?**

The Aatmas (loosely translated as souls) categorized under Kshara Purusha are not the same; there is a gradation (Taratamya in Sanskrit) in them. To put it in simple terms, Aatmas (also called consciousness) are subtle entities, which can neither be burnt nor broken into pieces, neither drowned in any liquid nor be destroyed. That means Aatmas are immortal in nature.

However, the subtleness of the Aatmas varies from Aatma to Aatma or a group of Aatmas. The subtler the Aatma, the more potent or powerful it is. This is what is called "Aatma-gradation" and this subtleness of the Aatma is inherent in that Aatma and it cannot be changed. To explain in simple terms, philosophers devised the word - grades/ stages (Kaksha in Sanskrit) to categorize Aatmas.

So, Aatma or a group of Aatmas is always on various Kakshas (imaginative steps of a ladder which determine the potency* or power of an Aatma and the inherent attributes they possess). These gradations are inherent in the Aatmas and not subject to change.

For instance, an Aatma that is in Kaksha 5 can never move into Kaksha 4 or Kaksha 6.

So, every Aatma or a group of Aatmas in a Kaksha will have a different potency compared to that of another Kaksha. The Aatmas on the lower Kaksha like "9", "10", "11" for example, are far less potent when compared to those on the higher Kaksha like "3", "4","5".

Subtler the Aatma, more attributes it has. Again, these attributes can be positive or negative. Positive ones support/ aid the laws of nature and the negative ones disturb/ block the laws of nature.

Since Brahman is infinitely subtle or infinitely subtler than any of the subtle entities in the material and spiritual worlds, HE is infinitely powerful. HIS attributes are always positive and are infinite in nature. This is the truth and it will always remain so until eternity. That's the reason why Brahman has no parallels at all and will always be so in the future too.

Another Aatma, which is categorized as Akshara Purusha, the one that is feminine in nature, named as Lakshmi in the scriptures – the Vedas & Upanishads, etc. is energy too. She is in a class of her own and is subtler than all the other Aatmas or energies classified under Kshara Purusha. Hence, she is highly potent and powerful, having more positive attributes than all other Aatmas put-together and has no negative attributes at all. She is still marginally inferior to Brahman.

Brahman is infinitely subtler than Lakshmi and hence infinitely more powerful and knowledgeable than her. Other than these two, all other Aatmas are graded; let's understand in brief how they are graded. But before that let's know the names of various Aatmas.

**List of Aatmas on various Kakshas**

Vedanta - scriptures like Vedas, Upanishads, Puranas, Bhagavata, etc. talk about Aatmas and their unique eternal names and their gender. They (scriptures) talk about the relationships between the Aatmas too. The saint Madhvacharya has elaborated the concept of Aatma gradation, through many of his works. One of such works is "Rigbhashya" – a collection of detailed commentaries on "Aiteraya", "Taittariya", "Brihadaranyaka", "Shatprashna", "Kena" and "Kathaka" Upanishads.

Also, scriptures like "Bhavishotara Purana" and "Garuda Purana" talk about gradations of Aatmas.

Brahman/ Narayana/ Vishnu is on the topmost Kaksha, that is "1", HIS eternal consort Lakshmi is on infinitely distant second Kaksha, that is "2", indicating she is infinitely inferior to him.

The Aatmas under Kshara Purusha are further classified as Devathas - demigods, Rishis - sages, Vasus, Rudras, Kinnaras, Yakshas all the way down, to the Aatmas grouped under Maanavas - humans. This list of Aatmas and the Kakshas are as follows.

| Kaksha Number | Name of the individual Aatma OR group of Aatmas |
|---|---|
| 1 | Brahman/ Narayana/ Vishnu – Lord of the Universe and beyond |
| 2 | Lakshmi – External consort of Narayana |
| 3 | (a) Chaturmukha Brahma (CB),<br>(b) Mukhya Prana Vayu (MPV) |
| 4 | (a) Saraswati – eternal consort of CB<br>(b) Bharathi – eternal consort of MPV |
| 5 | (a) Garuda<br>(b) Sesha<br>(c) Rudra |
| 6 | Shanmahishi-s of Krishna<br>(a) Jaambavati<br>(b) Bhadra<br>(c) Neela<br>(d) Kalindi<br>(e) Mitravinda<br>(f) Lakshana |
| 7 | (a) Sauparni – eternal consort of Garuda<br>(b) Vaaruni – eternal consort of Sesha<br>(c) Paarvati - eternal consort of Rudra |
| 8 | (a) Indra (Purandara)<br>(b) Kaama |
| 9 | Ahankaarika Prana |
| 10 | a) Svaayambhu Manu<br>b) Daksha Prajapati<br>c) Bruhaspatyacharya<br>d) Shachi - eternal consort of Indra (Purandara)<br>e) Rati – eternal consort of Kaama<br>f) Aniruddha – eternal son of Kaama |

This list can be endless since the countless Aatmas of living beings on the planet has to be on any Kaksha, either on its own or with other Aatmas.

Let us stop the list at 10, as listing the complete Aatma gradation is beyond the scope of the topic that we have begun to discuss.

***Potency-**  It is nothing but the mental power of an Aatma, which drives the body to do physical work and this, in turn, depends on the Kaksha it is placed in and vice versa. Lower the Kaksha, lesser the mental power** of the Aatma.

Always, the mind drives the body and a strong mind can make the body strong to win anything. That means, a strong mind leads to a strong determination, which in turn makes the body strong to give a "knock out" punch to an opponent inside the boxing ring. In any boxing competition, it is not the man with a strong (muscular) body who wins; it is rather the man with a strong mind and super determination who wins over the other. So, it is a game of the mind, not the game of muscle. This is true of every game/ sports.

We see the mind taking centre stage quite often in our day-to-day lives. Any work we start with a strong mind to finish will get completed, no matter how much physical toil it requires.

Do all Aatmas have the same kind of mental power? – NO. The Holy Scriptures say that the mental power is not the same as everyone. It depends on which Kaksha the Aatma is in. Higher the

Kaksha, more the mental power, for example - Brahman OR Narayana at Kaksha 1 has a mind that is infinitely powerful. So, it is quite obvious that HE is infinitely strong and powerful. Also, the knowledge or wisdom or the intellectual power of an Aatma depends on which Kaksha he/ she is in. Aatmas at the higher Kakshas are always intelligent and more capable than those at the lower Kakshas. So, Brahman being at the highest Kaksha makes HIM Infinitely intelligent or knowledgeable. So, it is obvious that HE creates, sustains and destroys the Universe and other subtle worlds at his will.

**mental power-There is much more than the mental power which determines the potency but for the common man to understand, I have not elaborated much, so as to avoid the confusion.

# Divine Aatmas (Energies)

## Introduction to divine Aatmas

Though there are countless numbers of Aatmas under the KP category, only those divine Aatmas, which are on the higher side of the Kaksha are able to execute the universal level activities. Their activities are classified into 2 levels-

## Macro-level

The activities inside and outside of these cosmic bodies of the all-encompassing Universe are countless and infinite in the truest sense.

Example: Let's consider our solar system, which has 9 planets revolving around the sun. They spin on their own vertical axis too. The divine energies mentioned earlier, take care of all the events also (from the atomic level to galactic level) within these planets. The activities extend and spread throughout the infinitely vast Universe. Since it is humanly impossible to comprehend and list out the entire cosmic activities for our discussion, we shall limit it only to the planet earth. Within the planet earth, let us limit the discussion only to a few macro and micro level activities, to understand better.

## Micro-level

There are 8.4 million living species on the planet earth and these divine Aatmas handle every activity inside these species. Since it is humanly impossible to decipher and understand the micro level activities too, let's limit to a few activities pertaining to human beings, to understand the truth better. Let us discuss it a bit later.

## Divine energies

The following is the list of divine energies:

- Chaturmukha Brahma

    He is responsible for the creation of the entire material universe.

- Vishnu

    He is Brahman himself and is the sustainer of the Universe until the end, in the macro world. In the micro world, HE is the inner dweller of every living being, giving life to it and oversees every activity happening inside the body. HE is the inner dweller inside every demigod too.

- Rudra

    Rudra is the destroyer of the Universe at the time of Universal dissolution in the macro world and in the micro world, HE is the power behind the working of the mind in every animal, including humans. A man's mood swings are at the discretion of Rudra.

- <u>Mukhya Prana - MP</u>

    Scriptures talk about the Universe with her countless astral bodies resting on "Vataavaran". "Vata" in Sanskrit means the wind and "Avaran" means sheath. So, a "sheath of wind" is holding these astral bodies - the gigantic cosmos, together, intact in the empty space. This sheath of wind is high potency energy, which is the manifestation of Mukhya Prana.

    At the macro level (Universal level), MP functions as "Vataavaran" and at the micro level, the same MP works as a life force, residing in every living being. A living being is said to be alive and kicking as long as He (MP) resides in its heart.

    The scripture like "Brahma-sutras" declares that whoever knows MP well, knows Vedas well. The MP or simply Prana is considered to be the breath of the Universe. Prana is the sum total of all energies that is manifested in the universe. It is the sum total of all the forces in nature.

Heat, light, electricity, magnetism, etc. are the manifestations of Prana. It further manifests in Pancha Pranas and Pancha upa-Pranas.

- Pancha Pranas

    Names of Pancha Pranas are as follows

    (a) Prana

    (b) Apana

    (c) Samana

    (d) Vyana

    (e) UdanaPancha upa-Pranas

- The 5 upa-Pranas (sub-Pranas) are as follows

    (a) Naga

    (b) Kurma

    (c) Krikala

    (d) Devadatta

    (e) Dhananjaya

Prana along with other 4 Pranas represent Pancha (five in English) Prana, as they take up all jobs in the micro and macro worlds. For example:

**Prana**: Is responsible for breathing out and Apana is responsible for breathing in. All the activities, which happen above the "belly button" in the human body are credited to Prana. The activities, which happen on the face – speaking, breathing, smelling, hearing, seeing, tasting, etc. happen due to the grace of Prana. Other than these, the beating of the heart and the functioning of lungs, the nervous system and brain cells, blood circulation to all the cells and organs above the belly button happen with the help of Prana.

**Apana**: Is responsible for all the activities below the "belly button" in the human body including excretion of indigested food. Apana too governs our reproductive activities. Also, all the activities we perform from the time we wakeup in the morning till we sleep in the night, happen because of Apana. This excludes those happening in the face.

**Vyana**: Is responsible for bringing movements in us. If we are able to walk, jump, run, dance, bend, swim, etc. it is because of the presence of Vyana in our bodies. The Vyana, by being at every joint, makes our joint movements a child's play to us. If in case Vyana is not working properly in our body, we experience joint(s) pain, which retards the body movements.

**Samana**: Is responsible for the segregation of nutrition from the food we consume and assimilate the same to the cells throughout the body. So, because of Samana, the right nutrition reaches the right cell. If we are healthy or diseased, the credit or blame should go to Samana.

**Udana**: Is responsible for the movement of Aatma out of the body, at the time of our death. When one has done good karma throughout by leading a spiritual life, his Aatma moves out from the upper part of the body above the belly button. When his good deeds reach the pinnacle, his Aatma moves out of the body piercing the Sahasrara chakra (crown chakra). It is an indication of his escape from the cycle of death and birth permanently and he is now ready for Moksha.

If one has done bad karma, one's Aatma goes out of the body from anywhere below the belly button. If one's deeds are of the lowest grade, his Aatma will move out of the body through the rectum or urinary area.

Also, Udana brings about communication and expression in humans. If Udana energy is rightly activated in someone, the person will be an excellent communicator; else his speech will be disjointed and less articulated. Udana is the one, which will let the individual experience the inner bliss.

Udana is the channel that leads from lower to upper levels of consciousness, carrying the energy of Kundalini—the dormant energy awakened through yoga practice. Udana energy is directly under the supervision of MP, which in turn is actively supervised by Brahman.

In a nutshell, our evolution from animal instincts to divine instincts is only because of Udana. To put it simply, we achieve divinity in life due to Udana.

There are 49 Pranas with MP leading the pack. The Pranas, which operate in the macro world, are called "Vayus" and those that operate inside the micro world are called "Pranas".

If the above 10 mentioned Pranas are responsible for activities in the micro world, the 37 other Vayus are responsible for various activities in the macro world. The Vayu by the name "Pravaha Vayu" co-ordinates and gets the works done through the 37 Pranas in the macro world. In the micro world, the Prana by the name "Aham Prana" supervises the 10 Pranas mentioned above, to get the various activities done through them in the micro world. MP supervises and controls both Pravaha Vayu and Aham Prana and their activities, by residing inside them.

**Other Aatmas behind the macro & micro level functions**

Apart from the Aatmas described above, there are many Aatmas on the Kaksha, at relatively lower grades contributing to the activities at the macro and micro levels. Let's take a few examples:

**Aditya**: Is the Aatma/ demigod/ energy behind the shining of Soorya (Sun in English). Aditya is the inner dweller of the cosmic Sun, radiating "the most important" solar energy, which is quintessential for life to sustain on planet earth. He is the demigod of day, the light. There are other energies at the higher Kakshas, which are also at play behind the working of Sun.

In the micro world, the same Aditya is responsible for the functioning of the right eye in every living being on earth. Along with Chandra and Swayambhuva Manu, he makes living beings see. So, if any living being is able to see, the credit should go to Aditya and the other two, who are the forces behind the eyesight.

**Chandra**: If the earth is able to balance on its axis while spinning and revolving around the sun, it is due to the presence of moon and its rotation around the earth. There is a demigod/ energy called "Chandra", residing inside the moon and makes it function systematically the way it should. This is in the macro world.

In the micro world, the same Chandra along with dighdevatas* are the forces behind the functioning of ears in the living beings. The demigod Chandra and dighdevatas* make living beings hear and interpret the sound waves coming from all the directions. He along with Swayambhuva Manu is also responsible for the functioning of the left eye.

**Varuna**: Varuna, in the macro world, is the resident deity of water and the demigod of oceans, seas and water bodies on the planet earth and also demigod of celestial oceans. He is the force behind the functioning of oceans, seas, rivers and other water bodies. He is one of the dighdevatas* representing 'west'. Dighdevatas* are demigods of directions (north, south, east and west).

In the micro world, Varuna helps living-beings grasp the taste of the food they eat and give the pleasure of eating. Sitting in the human tongue of two inches by five inches in dimension, He helps it grasp and distinguish millions of tastes. Even the slightest change in the taste of food, a human tongue can easily figure out. That's the power of Varuna.

**Indra**: Indra is the demigod and king of heavens. He is also the king of all other demigods. In the macro world, he is the force behind rains on the planet earth. All activities - cloud formation, low-pressure build-up, movement of clouds from high-pressure to low-pressure and from low temperature to the high-temperature areas, etc. happen because of him. This is how Indra is responsible for bringing rains across the world. He is the dighdevata* of the east.

In the micro world, he controls all sensory organs and also the human hands. If a man is able to sculpt, carve and create the most scintillating art, the credit should go to Indra. Similarly, if a man can write, draw pictures using his hands, the credit should go to Indra. Also, Indra along with Kaama - another demigod, is responsible for controlling the mind.

**Agni**: Agni is the demigod/ Aatma of fire. He is the heat behind the fire in the macro world. However, in the micro world, He along with other demigods like Vyana, Svaahadevi, Paarvati, and Saraswati are the forces behind communication in all the living beings. Living beings, be it insects or birds or animals or humans, communicate among themselves. Agni and other demigods facilitate that. If someone is speaking, it can be easily deduced as the combined powers at play. He is also one of the dighdevatas representing southeast.

**Ashwini Devatas** (AD): They are the celestial doctors who are responsible for the upkeep of health of demigods in the macro world.

In the micro world, AD and Pravaha Vayu (PV) are the forces behind the proper functioning of the nose. Living beings are able to grasp and differentiate over million different kinds of smell and it is possible only because of AD and PV.

There are many demigods/ Aatmas/ energies contributing to the working of Universe at the macro and micro levels simultaneously. Higher the Aatma at the Kaksha, more powerful it is, so the Aatma will have more responsibilities.

## Do human Aatmas have the gradation?

Human Aatmas too are on various Kakshas either individually or in groups and hence have the gradation. However, they are at significantly lower Kakshas, hence their potentials are far lesser than that of demigods.

In our day-to-day lives, we will see some people doing phenomenal work in their lifetime. They accomplish things, which we feel humanly not possible. On the contrary, some really struggle to do anything significant in life.

Why is it so? The answer lies in the Aatma's potency, which is determined by the Kaksha on which the Aatma exists. Let's list a few of such achievers:

- **Swami Vivekananda (SV)** - A 19th-century ascetic who introduced Hinduism to the west.
- **Ramakrishna Paramahamsa** – Guru of Swami Vivekananda, who inspired SV to achieve what he achieved in his life.
- **Subhash Chandra Bose** – Freedom fighter who assembled an indigenous army to rid India of British occupation.
- **Mahatma Gandhi** – The man who introduced "Non-Violence" into the Indian freedom struggle and went on to become Mahatma (great in Sanskrit).
- **Rajaraja Chola 1** – The Tamil emperor who ruled between 985 CE and 1014 CE, is considered to be one of India's greatest emperors who ruled over entire South India, Sri Lanka, and the

Maldives. He built "Brihadeeswarar temple", which is considered an architectural marvel even today.

- **Ashoka** – He was one of India's foremost emperors who ruled almost the entire Indian landmass between BCE 268 to BCE 232. Later on, he converted to Buddhism and propagated it all over South East Asia, East Asia, and Sri Lanka.

There are many more people like them around the world, who looked like ordinary humans but did extra-ordinary things in life, which an ordinary man can only envy of. Their outstanding contribution is due to the surprisingly high potential they had, which in turn depended on the relatively high Kaksha they existed on.

## Man is influenced by divine and evil energies

A man comes not only under the influence of divine energies but also under asuric (evil) energies all the time. Divine energies influence the human mind and intellect (Buddhi in Sanskrit) to think and do good things, driven by the right wisdom. However, asuric energies do the opposite. They spoil the human mind by filling it with lust, greed, jealousy, anger, and revenge taking thoughts. They spoil the right wisdom with logic, which justifies their so-called evil actions.

The issue is, if not checked, the actions performed under the influence of evil forces will generate negative karma and man has to pay for it, as it (negative karma) attaches to him even though some evil forces made him commit the sins.

So, it is important to know who these negative forces are, how they operate on the human mind and how they make humans perform evil actions. Let's take a brief look at the asuric energies next.

*Dighdevatas: Sanskrit word "digh" is loosely translated in English as direction. There are devtas, which represent the directions. The directions and their demi gods are as follows:

- Uttara (North) - Kubera – Kaksha 18
- Ishanya (North East) – Rudra – Kaksha 5
- Poorva (East) – Indra – Kaksha 8
- Agneya (South East) – Agni – Kaksha 15
- Dakshina (South) – Yama – Kaksha 12
- Nairutya (South West) – Nirutti – Kaksha 17
- Paschima (West) – Varuna - Kaksha 13
- Vayuvya (North West) – Pravaha Vayu – Kaksha 11

Each of the 8 directions has its own characteristics fulfilled by the presiding deity mentioned above. The Northern and Southern directions, house two poles of the magnetic energy, which keeps the planet earth on its axis. The demigods – Kubera and Yama are responsible for it.

The magnetic force of the Earth always flows from north to south vertically, while rain bearing clouds move from east to west. The directions keep the earth spinning from the east to west, which results in the phenomena like sunrise and sunset - day and night. Also, the directions play a very important role in the functioning of our planet, as they contribute to the seasonal changes. In a way, directions aid life on earth. Humans move from one place to another with the help of directions. We are able to pinpoint the location of any object on planet earth because of the same. The modern communications, GPS, transportation, etc. happen because of the directions.

## Shimshumara – the center of the Universe:

The philosophers of the yore have been saying that the Universe is not infinitely wide, as it has curvy boundaries. However, the free space beyond the boundaries is infinite (limitless). In fact, the Holy Scriptures say there is a space in the Universe called "Shimshumara", which they claim is the center of the Universe. The Universe appears like a giant wheel with curvy edges and infinite diameter. All the cosmic bodies like stars, galaxies, dark matters, planets, asteroids, etc. form the spoke of the wheel. As per Vedanta, the center of such a Universal wheel at which all spokes meet is called Shimshumara. Lord Narayana is present at the center by name Shimshumara and powers it. He has been spinning the wheel of Universe since the time it was created and spins it till the time the Universe gets totally annihilated during the Universal Dissolution. Since the entire Universe is like a gigantic wheel, it is symbolically represented as "Sudharshan Chakra" – the disk that Krishna used during the Mahabharata times, some 5000 years ago, to kill his adversaries. The spinning of the Universal wheel by Lord Narayana, an incarnation of Lord Krishna himself, symbolically represents bringing all the activities in the insentient Universe (from micro to macro levels) by HIM.

This Universal wheel is also called "Kalachakra" – wheel of time. The philosophers say the wheel of time brings the change in everything within the Universe. This change is also called as "ageing" by the thinkers. This wheel of time spares nothing from ageing because, whatever is created has to get destroyed one day, after the purpose of its creation is served. In fact, this wheel ensures it and Krishna in the Bhagavad Geeta (BG) states that HE is that Kalachakra. **Dhruva Nakshatra – North Star**. Krishna in the BG states that of all the stars HE is **"Dhruva Nakshatra" – the North Star.** This is due to the fact that the star is located near Shimshumara and because of that it gets prominence. The North Star is also called the center of the Universe.

## The Universe has directions

With the identification of the center and the boundaries of the Universe, it is easy to calculate the diameter of the same. When the center and the boundaries of the Universe are present, then there are directions too.

Since the Universe has 8 directions (digh in Sanskrit), the location of each and every object across the Universe can be identified and tagged. The directions of the movement of all the moving objects in the space can also be ascertained. The dighdevatas make all these happen.

The cosmos appears to be chaotic to our naked eyes and to our inferior mind but in reality, there is orderliness in the way the Universe functions.

## Asuric Aatmas - Evil energies

### Introduction

There are Aatmas with asuric (evil) qualities in the Universe, which are opposite to the divine. Their qualities are violence, lustfulness, arrogance, ignorance, greediness, selfishness, lack-of-right-knowledge, etc. They try to oppose the "law of nature". Some of these Aatmas have universal potencies with the reach of the macro and micro worlds. For example, they can influence the working of the Universe in the macro world and the working of minds in the micro world. That means, they have the ability to disturb the working of the Universe and at the same time, they have an influence on the living beings. Few other asuric Aatmas have a reach only within the micro world.

That means, the human mind and intellect come under the influence of these Aatmas in doing unethical things. These asuric Aatmas bring "animal instinct" in humans, which make them (humans) behave like animals at times and commit sins.

Divine Aatmas too influence the human mind and intellect, which results in humans performing pious actions. If "divinity" is the nature of the divine Aatmas, "evilness" is the nature of the asuric

Aatmas. So, they are 180 degrees (poles) apart and never the twain shall meet. Let's understand the nature of the Aatmas briefly.

### **Nature of Aatmas**

Aatmas can be loosely compared to the seeds of various plants. Like any plant-seed has its own nature, an Aatma too has its own intrinsic nature.

For example - The tamarind seed when sown and watered, it will only yield tamarind fruit when it is fully grown into a fruit-bearing tree. No matter how much we pour orange or mango juice or sugarcane juice to the root of the tamarind tree, it still yields tamarind fruit. This is because yielding tamarind fruit is the nature of the tamarind seed so it can never change.

It goes the same with mango seeds or soy or rice grains or any other plant seeds. This is because the nature of the seed is inherent to the seed itself. Like we cannot change or separate the sweetness from sugarcane, bitterness from bitter gourd and sourness from lemon, we can't make a mango tree yield an apple. Nature of a fruit is intrinsic to the fruit itself.

This is true with the nature of Aatmas too. We have seen in our lives that some people never want to harm anyone, despite being harmed by others. These people always wish good to even the troublemakers. They always think and do good to others; they never think of doing anything evil in their lives.

On the contrary, some people thrive by annoying others. They are sadistic as they derive pleasure out of others' sufferings. They are jealous and can't tolerate others' progress in life and are selfish to the core.

Why do these people behave like this? – The answer is, their behaviour is based on their nature, which is innate and can never-ever change.

## **Gradation of asuric Aatmas**

We have seen that all Aatmas categorized under the Kshara Purusha (KP) have gradation based on their potential to perform various activities. This, in turn, depends on the subtleness of the individual Aatma. Based on their intrinsic qualities, they are further classified as devas (divine Aatmas) or daityas (evil Aatmas). Earlier, we had seen the gradation of divine Aatmas under KP based on their inbuilt divine potential. Now, we shall see the gradation of asuric Aatmas based on their inherent evil potential – how evil the individual or group of Aatmas is. These Aatmas too have gender and individual names like the divine Aatmas. We are considering a few here, to keep the narration simple.

| Sl No | Name of the Aatma | Brief description |
|---|---|---|
| 1 | Kalee (Male) | Infinitely evil. He was born as Duryodhana during Mahabharata times and was killed by Bhīma, 2nd of the 5 Pandava kings. |
| 2 | Alakshmi | Eternal wife of Kalee, 100 times less evil than him. She was born as Manthara during the times of Rama. |
| 3 | Viprachitti (male) | He is 100 times less evil than Alakshmi. He was incarnated as Jarasandha during Krishna's time. Bhīma killed him. |
| 4 | Kaalnemi (Male) | He is 100 times less evil than Viprachitti. He was born as Kamsa during Krishna's times and was slained by Krishna himself. |
| 5 | Madhu & Kaitab (male) | Both are 5 times less evil than Kaalnemi and were slayed by Vishnu |
| 6 | Alia Viprachitti (female) | Eternal wife of Viprachitti, She is 5 times less evil than Madhu, Kaitabh |
| 7 | Narakasur (Male) | He is 5 times less evil compared to Aila Viprachitti. He was born as Narakasura during Krishna's time and was killed by Krishna himself. |

There are many more Daitya Aatmas in the Universe, which try to oppose the law of nature, creating chaos. One such incident (disturbing the Universal order) occurred in the first Manvantara* called "Swayambhuva Manvantara". A Daitya by name Hiranyaksha pushed the earth away from its axis, approximately 1 billion years ago. His intention was to destroy the planet earth itself. It was Lord Vishnu who incarnated as "Koorma" - a wild boar and killed the Daitya, brought the earth back to its axis and restored the Universal order.

## The battle between asuras and devas

The battles between the evil forces (dark energies) and divine forces (white energies) have been happening from the time immemorial, in the mortal and celestial worlds. The divine forces or the demigods with the help of Lord Vishnu (Brahman) win over the dark forces all the time. In the mortal world, these asuric Aatmas take to human form and mercilessly wage mass atrocities against people – men, women, and children. They (evil Aatmas) even influence the human mind and intellect, instigating them to do bad things to the mankind. Their instigation results in massive destruction. The world has seen various wars for the last few millennia but from the last 1000 years, wars and the destructions have been recorded. All these wars and the pain they (evil forces) cause are due to their sadistic tendencies. The divine forces too take human-form and counter-influence the human minds, to resist and fight back the evil people. In the ensuing war, millions get erased from the face of the earth. At least they (divine energies) check the brutality of evil forces first and win over them ultimately. In the end, "truth triumphs" and the universal order is restored.

The asuric Aatmas always strive to take control of the Universe – mortal and celestial worlds and lord over them. If they are unable to do so, it is because of Brahman, who, through various divine incarnations, stop them from doing that. That's exactly the reason why the evil Aatmas detest Vishnu.

## Mahabharata – the war of worlds

The epic Mahabharata war (MW) was the war of worlds – good against evil, divine against asuric forces and white against dark forces. In fact, the MW was the first war the world has ever witnessed where multinational armies fought and slaughtered each other to death. The total number of men exterminated in 18 days of the war was over 50 lakhs (5 million). No war on earth has ever seen these kinds of gruesome killings in such a short period of time.

What makes MW an epic? – The war saw the participation of who's who of the Daityas led by Kalee– the ultimate in the evil spirit, incarnated as Duryodhana fighting against the divine forces (the incarnation of demigods), led by Lord Krishna himself.

The evil forces led by Duryodhana wanted to siege control of the world and rule in an adharmic (non-righteous) way. Lord Krishna countered his plan and his efforts by killing him and other asuras through Pandavas and other warrior kings. Thus the dharma – righteousness was established in the end.

**Do ordinary humans have the ability to influence others?**

Human Aatmas have limited ability to influence others' minds. This is because humans face a serious limitation - an individual can't exist in more than one place at any given time. This is unlike the divine and asuric Aatmas, that too at higher Kakshas, who can be at many places at any given time. So, they can be physically present in the celestial worlds and yet influence humans and other living beings on the earth. They do it by getting inside the human intellect and mind as pure subtle energy and influence them (humans) directly. This is not possible for the ordinary humans, though there are a few exceptional humans who have done it through their yogic powers.

Let's briefly see how these Universal energies influence the human mind and intellect and drive them (humans) to perform actions.

## Universal energies control humans

We have read about divine and asuric Aatmas (energies in short) influencing every living being, including humans. Other than those, there are 3 more energies constantly influencing the living being. These 3 energies are associated with "moola prakritti" (MPR) – nature in the raw and abstract form after Universal dissolution. They are an integral part of MPR and they're always there since the beginning. The 3 energies are creative, sustenance and destructive energies and are involved in the creation, sustenance, and destruction of the Universe.

### Energies have Gunas

Guna of an object is loosely translated as the quality of its inbuilt nature. Guna is classified as Sathvik, Rajasik, and Tamasik. Energies too have these Gunas, as they are inherent to them (energies).

The creation is associated with Rajasik Guna, which is represented by a red colour.

The sustenance is associated with Sathvik Guna, which is represented by white colour. The destruction is associated with Tamasik Guna, which is represented by black colour.

These Gunas from nature constantly influence us in one-way or the other. They influence directly our mind and intellect directly. We have seen that in a day, our thoughts change so many times, which drive the changes in the mood too. So, mood swings happen because of our thoughts.

## **What drives our Manas?**

Many entities drive our Manas and among them, our sensory organs – eyes, ears, nose, tongue, and skin, contribute the most. The sensory organs command the Manas to serve them as a slave, irrespective of what our intellect says. We are in fact, the slaves of our Manas.

Also, we have seen some people who are diabetic tend to eat sweets and suffer even later. This happens despite the doctor's advice and the warnings from their own intellect. This is because they are unable to resist the temptation for sweets created by their tongues – one of the sensory organs.

Similarly, we end up doing things, which we are not supposed to do, in spite of the cautions we receive from our intellect, this is again due to the sensory organs controlling us.

Indriya Abhimani daityas (asuric Aatmas, who influence sensory organs at times) get inside our sensory organs and create cravings for material objects, which include gambling, consuming liquor and illegal sex. Sometimes these cravings will make us do unethical things in life and contribute to our negative karma.

However Indriya Abhimani devtas - divine Aatmas, who contribute to the working of the sensory organs, too drive our minds. But they influence our minds through good thoughts, which will eventually make us perform ethical actions. Our ethical actions add to positive karma.

Energies from MPr also influence us 24x7, so, constantly we are influenced to think and do good OR bad things throughout lives based on our past Karmas. When our time for our eternal journey towards the Infinitely intelligent and powerful Lord Narayana arrives, Indriya Abhimani devtas influence our mind through sensory organs to think and do things, which will bring divinity in our life.

**The food we eat has a direct bearing on our mind**

Inside our stomach, there is a divine energy called Vaishvanara Agni that breaks down the food we consume into 3 parts.

- **Gross** – This is used to nourish the cells, which make up our muscle, organs, bones etc.

- **Subtle** – This is used to nourish bone marrow cells, nerve cells and other cells of the body which are subtler than the cells of muscle.

- **Subtlest** – This is used to nourish our mind, intellect, and memory (conscious and sub-conscious). So, the mind gets its feed from the food we eat thus supporting the adage – "We are what we eat".

- **Grossest** – The part of the consumed food which has no nutrition and difficult to digest, gets converted as "excreta" or the "fecal matter" and ejected out by inducing bowel movements.

## Food has Gunas:

The food we consume has Gunas, which influence our mind. The Gunas of the food are Sathvik, Rajasik, and Tamasik.

- **Sathvik food SF**

    It uplifts the mind OR mood towards the infinity and brings joy in us to keep us energized and happy. SF not only nourishes our body but also feeds our minds with good, constructive and divine thoughts. SF keeps us physically active in life.

- **Rajasik food RF**

    This food is not as nourishing to the body as Sathvik food but brings in passions and negative thoughts to our mind.

Man gets the feelings of greed and selfishness due to this. The food makes him lazy and less active.

- **Tamasik food TF**

    This food malnourishes the body as it is difficult for digestion and assimilation to the body. The body gets even less nourished than RF and one will feel lazy to do any work. In addition to this, the mind gets flooded with the negative thoughts and also gets flooded with the feelings of greed, lust, and revenge-taking emotions. One will get arrogance and anger at the drop of the hat. In a nutshell, man gets animal instincts by consuming TF. The result of all these is high BP, diabetes, gastrointestinal, kidney disorders, acute weakness, malfunctioning of heart and finally cardiac arrests and death.

Consuming meat of any animal including fish in addition to onions and garlic induces Tamasik thoughts in our mind, which in turn moves our body to behave badly. The bad behaviour attracts criticism from people, which in turn pushes him towards the anger and rage. He can never be happy in life because of all these and the root cause of the problem is the food he consumes on a daily basis. So, Vedanta strongly pitches for "Sathvik food" to be consumed by all to stay healthy and happy.

## Effects of MPr induced Sathvik, Rajasik and Tamasik forces on humans

When a man is under strong the influence of Sathvik force of MPr, he will get active, will get duty bound, think and do well to others. He loves and respects all. He is always positive in his mindset.

The same person, when he is under the influence of a strong Rajasik force, feels greedy, gets very self-centered and is ready to do anything for personal glory and money. He is only after personal gratification seeking sensory pleasures.

When the person is under the influence of Tamasik force, inertia sets in; his greediness is boundless. Other than that, he is driven by negative thoughts and involves in harming others, taking pleasure out of others' sufferings.

However, the influences of these 3 energies are not permanently fixated on us, they keep changing. Sometimes Sathvik, sometimes Rajasik and some other times Tamasik forces act on us. It could last for a few hours in a day to a few days a month OR a few months a year.

## Aatmas have inbuilt Gunas

Every Aatma (which is pure energy in essence) has its own built-in Guna like other energies mentioned above. They are (a) Sathvik (b) Tamasik and (c) Mixture of both called Rajasik.

This implicit Guna along with the Gunas of the energies of MPr influence a person. In addition to these, there are other factors – circumstances in which he lives, works, the food he eats, etc. also shape his mind. So, if a person behaves in a way, it is these driving forces, which make him behave that way. After understanding the forces at play, blaming him for bad behaviour OR praising him for good behaviour seems a little childish.

**Our emotions have colours**

We know that matter has colour, but Vedanta says energies have colours too. The emotions inside our Manas and the knowledge we gained through Buddhi (intellect), which is stored in the conscious memory, are also subtle energies and hence have colour. The colour appears as aura, which can be captured by the Kirlian camera.

**Example**

When someone is happy and joyful the colour of the emotions in his Manas is golden yellow. This colour shows up on his face subtly.

When someone is angry, his emotion in his Manas turns red, so his face turns red.

When someone is disappointed in life and sad, the emotion in his Manas turns light brown, so it shows up on his face.

When one's knowledge of any subject is deep, his body produces a blue aura. When he has no depth in any subject, just a superficial person, then the body oozes out brown aura.

This is exactly the reason why in Hinduism the bodies of Lord Krishna and Lord Rama – avatars of the Brahman are depicted in deep blue colour in the altars. The deep blue colour represents the infinite knowledge they have about everything plus they still remain a mystery to everyone. No one could understand them fully so far, as they are beyond our intellects to decipher.

### **Aatma being energy has colour too**

Every Aatma is energy by itself and hence has colour. The colour of an Aatma is tied to its inherent Guna (Sathvik, Rajasik & Tamasik) and where it is located on the Kaksha.

- Sathvik Guna is pure white
- Rajasik Guna is pure red
- Tamasik Guna is pure black.

Higher the Kaksha, more Sathvik is the Guna of the Aatma, so its colour is whiter, indicating purer. So Chaturmukha Brahma (CB), Mukhya Prana (MP) have the whitest colour of all Aatmas because they are in the 3rd Kaksha. The Aatmas of the 4th Kaksha, Saraswati and Bharathi have the energy, which is a lesser shade of white than that of CB and MP. Less the Sathvik and more of Tamasik means, the energy of the Aatma turns blackish white.

More the Rajasik, less Sathvik means, the energy of the Aatma turns reddish white. It goes on like this until it becomes pure red and pure black when the Guna of the Aatmas are fully Rajasik and Tamasik respectively.

## Intelligent forces behind every activity

There are intelligent forces behind every activity happening in the Universe. If we look at our planet itself, we see many celestial activities, for example –

Sunrise & sunset, waxing & waning of the moon, the monsoons, seasons, eclipses (lunar & solar), etc. happen with such a precision, that it astonishes everyone. To top it all, nature makes everything mesmerising – the mountains, the oceans, the ripple sound of the rivers, the monsoons (soothing sound of rains), the seasons, the forests, the cool breeze, the animal kingdom, the taste of seasonal fruits and the scent of flowers, the melodious chirping of birds, so on and so forth. These inspire an ordinary person to turn into a creative poet.

There is a melody in the various sounds of nature, which narrates her story in a musical way through different rhythms. So, from the time immemorial, writers, thinkers, musicians, philosophers, scientists, inventors, innovators and others have turned to nature, to get inspiration for their work and it is that magnificent.

Let's consider the phenomena like sunrise and sunset, which give rise to day and night. However, the work involved in bringing about these events day-in-day-out is not easy. It is too complicated and cannot happen on its own. How can the earth spin without any flaws so accurately from the time it was created, over 2 billion years ago? No wear and tear or whatsoever have ever been recorded. The earth never spins faster OR slower. Once started, it has been spinning over and over again at a constant speed and that is the beauty of it.

The solar energy emanating from the sun, the earth spinning on its axis and orbiting around the sun, are the reasons why we have the phenomena like day and night, waxing and waning of the moon, cloud formation & monsoons, the seasons, etc. They are in turn responsible for life on the planet.

How do all the celestial events happen day-in-day-out so precisely? There are intelligent energies, which make things happen. These intelligent energies are demigods and they are behind these superbly coordinated events.

### **Demigod Chandra behind the functioning of the moon**

Our planet earth has one natural satellite – moon, which revolves around the earth once every 27.4 days. We know the earth moves on its axis around the sun and it is very important for the earth to be on its axis forever, else it may go and bang against other planets or go away towards the sun only to get burnt off.

What is keeping the earth fixated on its axis? – The Moon. The earth is keeping the moon fixed to its axis too. Both are mutually helping each other to be on their respective tracks. Also, waves in the oceans on the earth are because of the orbiting of the moon around the earth.

The demigod Chandra, who is also called Soma, is the energy behind the working of the Moon. Following are the responsibilities of Chandra in the macro and micro world

Roles of demigod Chandra are as follows

## **Macro world**

### The deity of Vanaspathi

He is the Deity of vegetation. He nurtures the vegetation during the night. Whatever nutrition is generated through sunlight is maintained and nurtured by Soma during the night so that vegetation loses no nutrition. However, during the day the sun will take care of it (vegetation) through photosynthesis.

## The deity of Anna

He is the Deity of food – everything to do with eating and drinking. He is the one that nurtures the body of living beings.

## Microworld

### Hearing

The energy behind the working of ears in the human body

### Seeing

The energy behind the functioning of left eyes in humans

### Thinking

Human thinking has many energies working behind it. There are other energies, which are on the higher Kakshas that make the mind to function as it should.

## Demigod Vivasvan behind the functioning of the sun

The solar system is generally called the sun and its debris. This is because compared to the sun, the other planets look so tiny and are mistaken to be the debris of it.

To illustrate the comparative sizes of the sun and the other planets, if we consider the sun, for example, it is as big as a soccer ball and the planet Jupiter – largest planet in the solar system, is as big as a lemon. The other bigger planets are of the size of peanuts, while the size of the earth can be compared to a mustard seed. The size of the earth is insignificant when compared to that of the sun.

All planets with their satellites orbiting them, march to revolve around the sun. The sun itself along with the solar system is orbiting around the center of the Milky Way Galaxy (MWG) at a speed of 828000 KM/ hour. Yet, it takes approximately 300 million solar years to orbit once around the MWG. The MWG consists of billions of stars (bigger than our sun) and planets. What astonishes us the most is, the MWG is not even a blip in the universe. It appears just as a white dot on the telescope screen. Now, imagine how big and infinitely complex the Universe is! So, try imagining how mighty and complex is the creator – the Brahman!!

Let's come back to the solar system. The sun releases solar energy into the solar system and is the essence of life on the Earth. The main semi-divine energy behind the functioning of the sun is "Vivasvan", who is also called as "Aditya". However, Aditya gets his power from the indwelling deity "Surya Narayana" (SN), who is Brahman himself. In a nutshell, SN is the presiding deity who gives the solar power to the sun. The SN is pictorially depicted as the divine, riding a chariot of 7 horses, travelling from east to west. The seven horses represent the 7 colours of white light energy – Violet, Indigo, Blue, Green, Yellow, Orange and Red (VIBGYOR), the main solar energy behind the life on the planet earth.

Let us see what SN does in macro and micro worlds.

**Macro world**

Season formation

    Vivasvan along with 37 Vayus (wind currents) led by Pravaha Vayu (one more wind current, who supervises and controls the other 37 wind currents) brings seasons to earth.

Water evaporation

    During peak summer season, Vivasvan helps in evaporating the water from all the water bodies plus seas and oceans.

Cloud formation

    Vivasvan along with Varuna helps in the formation of water-bearing clouds.

Photosynthesis

    Vivasvan helps the vegetation to develop food through photosynthesis.

## Microworld

Seeing

>Vivasvan is behind the working of the right eye in the humans.
>
>There are many more tasks that Vivasvan does, coordinating with other demigods in the micro and macro worlds.

Let us look into the micro world to further delve into these intelligent and helping forces. What better way to do that, than investigating the human body and its functioning? - Millions of activities (subtle and gross) - from simple to the most complex ones happen inside the human body and these activities take place in a systematic manner to keep the body functioning normally and remain "hale and healthy". Let's analyze a few of such activities in brief and what drives them. Let's get to know the anatomy of the human body as per Vedanta.

## The human body and Pancha koshas

The human body is made up of Pancha (five in English) Koshas (loosely translated as the sheath in English). They are as follows:

- Annamaya Kosha
- Pranamaya Kosha
- Manomaya Kosha
- Vijnanamaya Kosha

- Anandamaya Kosha
- Annamaya Kosha-AK

The gross human body along with heart, lungs, kidneys, liver, bones and bone marrow, brain, nerves, stomach, small and large intestines, etc. form the Annamaya Kosha. It is a sheath of gross objects, which is visible to the naked eyes. But Annamaya Kosha is present, even in a dead body.

## **Pranamaya Kosha-PK**

This is the sheath of life force. When this sheath is active, the man starts breathing and is said to be alive. His body seems to be warm, due to the presence of "pranagni" – invisible fire in subtle form, which is linked to Prana or life. A man with only these two active sheaths is said to be in the unconscious state. This is because, he needs "Manas" – (loosely translated as the mind in English), to get into a conscious state.

## **Manomaya Kosha-MK**

This sheath encapsulates Manas, Buddhi – intellect, and Ahamkara – awareness of the self. When a man is said to be in the conscious state, he is able to see and talk to people. He can even think a bit. However, he is not aware of himself. He doesn't remember anything, as his memory shell is not active. So, he talks to people and forgets about them as soon as they go away from his sight. At this stage, he is still not a fully normal man as he is considered to be diseased mentally.

## Responsibilities of Manas, Buddhi, and Ahamkara

- **Ahamkara**

    This faculty brings the awareness of "I" to the individual. For a person to get the feeling "I am so and so", this should be activated, else he wouldn't know who he is. In a nutshell, "Ahamkara" answers the question "Who am I?"

- **Manas**

    Sensory organs (eyes, nose, ears, skin, and tongue) grasp the external information and send it to the Manas for further processing. The external information brings desire through emotions in the Manas and that's when the man wants whatever he has seen, heard about, touched, smelled and may be tasted too. But Manas can't take decisions, which is the responsibility of Buddhi. There are many demigods driving the Manas (starting from Parjanya – Kaksha 20, Agni – Kaksha 15, Chandra - Kaksha 12, Aniruddha – Kaksha 10, Indra – Kaksha 8, Kama – Kaksha 8, Rudra, Sesha, Garuda - Kaksha 5, CB and MP – Kaksha 3, Lakshmi – Kaksha 2 and Narayana – Kaksha 1).

- **Buddhi**

    Buddhi being the faculty of the intellect decides if whatever Manas desires, should it be pursued or not. Saraswati and Bharathi – Kaksha 4 are the demigods behind the working of Buddhi.

**Vijnanamaya Kosha-VK**

The inner faculty of MK is VK. This sheath encapsulates Chitta – (loosely translated as conscious memory)

The demigods responsible for the functioning of Chitta are Mukhya Prana and Chaturmukha Brahma – Kaksha 3. VK encapsulates Conscious memory (CM), which stores the information about things we use on a daily basis – work (office and home), information about all the people (friends, relatives, colleagues and known personalities) we interact regularly, information related to the food we commonly eat so on and so forth. Whatever information, we don't use regularly will be moved to the Subconscious mind (SCM). For example the names of our childhood friends – whom we used to regularly interact with in elementary/ primary school. We generally tend to forget their names, looks, and voice when we are adults if don't interact with them often. So, the information captured about our childhood friends is moved to SCM and never destroyed.

The reality is, our conscious mind never forgets anything. Once the information is captured, it is stored forever. If something is not stored in the CM, it means we haven't grasped it with full attention.

## Anandamaya Kosha - AK

The innermost faculty of MK is AK. This has Chetana – the expansion of CM, which is also called Subconscious Memory (SCM). The SCM is made of 3 compartments

- Compartment 1 to hold the past information

    This section has the repository of the information – people, places, and events across our current and past lives. It is so astonishing that such a small subatomic sized entity stores not only information about names of the objects but also taste, sound, smell, aroma etc. and also the events linked to them. For example, if someone has heard a sound of a musical note, which he feels, not heard in his entire lifetime, yet the note is somehow familiar to him. So, whenever he listens to that tune, he vaguely remembers, like in his dream that some incidents connected to the tune. That tune could be from one of his past lives and the incident could be that he met his beautiful girlfriend at the concert when the tune was being played in the background.

- Compartment 2 to hold all the past and the present Karmas

    There is a section that carries all the Karmic impressions of all our past and the present lives. Based on these impressions, we will either be born as humans OR animals OR worms OR insects OR reptiles etc.

- Compartment 3 to contain Instinct

    GOD has given each of us "Instinct", which is made up of beliefs. It is the responsibility of the instinct to protect us from every danger, as it believes we are alive and we should be kept safe and alive. For example, when we are walking in a street and if we hear a harsh sound of a falling object from the top, we tend to run helter-skelter. What made us run like this? – It is our "basic instinct". Our instinct will make us run away from the danger the moment it senses it. This is done in order to save us from death because our instinct believes we are alive and it does whatever required keeping us alive. So it is the responsibility of our instinct to save us from accidental deaths. On the contrary, if we go on programming our mind that we are dead, over a period of time, the Instinct of ours will start believing that we are dead. So someday, instinct will stop our heartbeat and kill us. In a nutshell, we GET what we continuously SAY OR THINK in life.

It is this instinct that the new age motivational speakers, psychologists ask us to make use of to get whatever we want in life. We have to note that our deep desires are preludes to our beliefs. It is our deep desires, which get transformed into beliefs and stay in on SCM. When the beliefs get strong enough, our instinct pulls whatever we desire from anywhere and hands it over to us. It could be wealth, health, happiness, just about anything.

The demigod responsible for the functioning of Chetana is Lakshmi – Kaksha 2, the eternal consort of Lord Narayana.

## **Tripurushas and the Pancha Koshas**

There are three Purushas – loosely translated as beings, who control the Pancha koshas.

- **Shareera Purusha -SP**

    Shiva of the Kaksha 4 is called as the SP who governs Annamaya Kosha, which is made up of earth and water. If Shiva's exclusive grace is there on any individual, that person will be in the pink of health. Grace happens only due to the good Karmic impressions of the past.

- **Chanda Purusha -CP**

    Sesha of the Kaksha 4 is called as the CP as he governs the Pranamaya Kosha, which is made up of air and fire. If Sesha's exclusive grace is present on any individual, whatever that individual says will be sensible and makes sense to the others. Also, the individual can go on to become an influential orator who can mesmerize others through his oratory skills. However, Sesha's exclusive grace can only happen when the individual deserves it.

- **Veda Purusha -VP**

    Garuda of the Kaksha 4 is called as the VP as he governs Manomaya Kosha and their inner faculties – Vijnanamaya Kosha & Anandamaya Kosha. If Garuda's exclusive grace happens to any individual, knowledge of the higher realm will begin to unravel to that person. The Vedas, which are considered to be the Holy Grail when it comes to describing the "indescribable GOD" – Brahman, is very difficult to comprehend. Every word of over a million words used in 3 Vedas – "Rig", "Yajur" and "Saama" has a minimum of 3 deeper meanings. Each of the deeper meaning is trying to convey the "unconveyable GOD" – Brahman. So, in a nutshell, it is humanly impossible to grasp the Vedas fully without the divine grace. When the time of an individual arrives to understand GOD to his capacity, Garuda's exclusive grace happens to him.

## Conscious memory - CM

All information related to one's day-to-day activities – events he attends or comes to know about, people he meets or knows about, other objects he experiences in life are stored in his conscious mind (CM). When he studies, his study related information; when working, his work-related information; the information about his family, friends, relatives, colleagues, neighbours, so on and so forth are all stored in his CM. He uses this information regularly in his day-to-day life. So, in a nutshell, CM stores information only about his present life.

When a man sees an apple fruit, he understands it as apple because he has seen/ eaten the apple fruit earlier and the information is recorded in the CM. The moment he sees the fruit, his mind compares the image captured by the eyes, with that of the information about the apple available in the CM. That's how he comes to the conclusion that what he is seeing is nothing but an apple fruit itself and that happens within microseconds.

## Subconscious memory -SCM

In contrast, the expansion of CM is SCM, which stores information across lives – past and present. Our past experiences – people with whom we interacted, the events we attended and much more across lives, are stored in the SCM. In fact, the SCM is a divine cassette that contains all the recorded information of our past lives. Sometimes, we come across people with familiar faces, not sure of where we have met/ seen them. It may not be in this life at all but it may be from our past lives. We must have interacted with similar looking people in our past lives. It's just that we don't remember or don't know how to access and play the recorded memories. Through deep meditation, if we are able to send our attention towards VK piercing other Koshas, we will able to unlock it. Let's look into a few stored details of the SCM.

- **Our beliefs stay in SCM**

    Example: - SCM stores everything across lives including a man's strong beliefs. That means, if a man strongly believes in telling the truth and leading an ethical life, he spends his life, living truthfully. His belief is recorded in the SCM and won't go away even when he dies. In his next human life, if he wants to deviate from the truth even temporarily, his conscience strongly opposes it and won't allow him to do so. Therefore, he sticks to the truth and leads life accordingly. This is the beauty of the SCM.

- **Life changing incidences stay in SCM**: -

    Example1: - SCM records gruesome incidences or events, which occurred in his present or past lives. For example, a person on his way home is waylaid and attacked by armed thugs who are hell bent to kill him and take away his money. If he escapes miraculously with or without money, it will be a big deal for him. However, the incident would shake his confidence in the core and the fear would grip his life and go straight to the SCM as a recording. Though the incident happened once in his life, it would trouble him throughout until death. This is due to the fact that the incident and the subsequent fear, both are etched in the SCM. It won't stop here, it will seep into his next life. In that life, he will have some kind of fear when he has to take a deserted road even during daytime. He feels uncomfortable due to anxiety, with the expectation of danger.

    Example 2: - A lady going late from office gets into a deserted lift. Let us hypothetically consider there is a power outage and in-between, she feels the presence of a ghost crying and laughing in the lift intermittently in the dark. She starts to shiver uncontrollably due to the fear and chillness inside.  Let's imagine she escapes from that incident and reaches home safely. But the incident creates a recording in the SCM permanently. She will forever have the fear of being alone, either at home or in the office, let alone taking a deserted lift. This fear strikes even in her next life, whenever she approaches a lift all alone. This is because of the past incident and the fear recorded in the SCM.

## Deep knowledge on any subject stays in our SCM

Deep knowledge gained out of lifelong contemplation, experimentation, research, scientific exploration and the like gets recorded in SCM, so is the information about music, deep philosophical insights, etc., for which a man has put in enduring and hard-hitting efforts to gain the knowledge.

- Example

    If someone has put-in lifetime efforts to understand astronomy and made decent progress in it, his deep knowledge of the subject will get recorded in his SCM. So, in his next human life, even during his juvenile age, the person will show an inclination towards astronomy and remembers all the formulas/ equations phenomenally well as if he has studied it yesterday. He will exhibit the qualities of a scientist at an early age itself, which is amazing.

This will happen to people proficient in any subject – music, philosophy, engineering, medicine, etc.

## **Our deep desires find its place in the SCM**

Example 1: A boy and girl are in love and their deep desire to marry remains unfulfilled due to either the boy or girl passing away or may be due to any other reason. If their desire is deep, it finds a place in the SCM. In their next human life, it doesn't matter in which part of the world the boy and girl are born, they somehow find a way to meet and fall in love again and finally marry. At last, their deep desire will get fulfilled making the boy and girl happy.

- Example2

    Someone has an intense desire to become a neurosurgeon in life and somehow could not accomplish it due to various reasons, including funds and dies one day, without turning his dream into reality, his desire remains recorded in his SCM and kept intact. In his next human life, this man will be able to implement his wish without much fuss. The divine creates an environment required for becoming a neurosurgeon, so things get easy for him. SCM also carries the fruits of Karma across lives.

Having known Pancha Koshas, now we shall briefly look at a few activities inside the human body and the smart energies, which make it happen.

## Annamaya Kosha

It relates to the entire gross body constituting the muscles, bones, bone marrows, lungs, heart, organs and the like.

Of all the activities that happen inside the human body, the beating of the heart is the foremost important because if someone's heart is beating, it indicates the person is alive. For every other activity to happen, the beating of the heart is a necessity or being alive is a must. That's the reason why we should look into Prana – the force of life first. The Prana keeps living beings alive. So, Prana belongs to Pranamaya Kosha – the sheath of life.

## Pranamaya Kosha – the brief introduction

Prana is the essence of life. If any creature is living, then it is breathing and with this one can infer that its Pranamaya Kosha is active.

Heartbeats and the very essence of life:

Mukhya Prana (MP) is the presiding deity of life. He resides in the heart of every living being and makes them breathe involuntarily, thus keeping them alive. In the human body too, he is at the heart, aiding heartbeats to keep the person alive.

- **We breathe 21,600 times an hour**

    Normally when we complete breathing 21,600 times, it is said that the body has aged by 24 hours. Ageing of the body is not linked to the external clock or calendar, which we are used to. Body's ageing is directly coupled with the number of times we breathe per second.

    Breathing 21,600 times in 24 hours calls for breathing once every 4 seconds on an average. At this rate, the biological clock is said to be in sync with the regular clock. So, when our body ages by 100 years, externally also 100 calendar years would have been passed.

    That means we would have breathed 21,600 x 365 x100 = 77, 76, 00,000 times when our body ages by 100 years. In our lifetime, we breathe seventy-seven crores, seventy-six lakh times. Our body is designed to function for these many heartbeats.

    Instead of breathing once every 4 seconds, if we are regular joggers and tend to breathe twice every 4 seconds, our body ages quickly. That means we would have already aged 100 years internally when the external calendar has turned just 50 years only. Hence, yoga, meditation, and Pranayama – the essence of the Vedantic way of living, all proscribe slower breathing for a long, healthy and happy life.

MP and other 11 Pranas (10 upa-Pranas supervised and controlled by Aham Prana) are the energies behind breathing and they keep the individual alive. In a way, they are responsible for ageing in all the living beings. They do it under the direct supervision of MP and Lord Narayana OR Brahman.

**The human body is mapped to Biological calendar**

Our inner body calendar has 360 days a year, unlike the external calendar, which depends on the time taken by the earth to orbit the sun once. So, 360 days when calculated for 100 years, it becomes 36,000 days. That means, 36,000 days and 36,000 nights. When they are added, it becomes 72,000 days and nights. This matches exactly with 72,000 nadis – subtle to gross nerves, which exist in our body. The 36,000 nadis lie on to the left side of the body and the remaining 36,000 lies on to the right side of the body. The Pranas move through these nadis up and down to keep the body hale and healthy. In case there is a distortion in their movements, the body attracts all kinds of diseases. However, the regular practice of Pranayama will make Pranas move through these nadis freely without any restriction, which will chase the diseases out and makes the body healthy. So, to remain fit and kicking, the regular practice of Pranayama is a must. Out of 72,000 nadis, 3 nadis are utmost important and they are "Ida", "Shushumna" and "Pingala". Ida nadi lies to the left side of the body. It is one of the 36,000 nadis representing night OR feminine side, which is also called intuitional side of humans. Pingala nadi is one of the 36,000 nadis representing day OR masculine side of the body, which is called as intellect OR logical side of humans. The Shushumna nadi lies in the center with 36,000 nadis on its left and right sides. It is through this nadi, the "Kundalini Shakti" – feminine serpent-power lying dormant at the "Mooladhara chakra" – base chakra, moves up when it gets energized and unites with "Shiva Shakti" at "SahasraHara chakra" – crown chakra. Also when a person dies and attains Moksha, his Aatma movies out of his body by piercing "SahasraHara chakra" through Shushumna nadi.

## How to delay aging?

Suppose, instead of breathing once every 4 seconds, if we delay our breathing to once every 8 seconds, automatically our body ages by 50 years, when the external clock or calendar turns 100 years. Though we lived for 100 years as per external calendar, our body would have aged just 50 years only as per our inner clock and feel as energetic as 50 years old. So, we would age 100 years internally, when the external clock has ticked away 200 years. That means the earth would have orbited the sun 200 times.

Similarly, if we breathe once every 16 seconds, our body will turn 100 when the external calendar turns 400 years. That means the earth would have orbited the sun 400 times. This way, we can delay ageing and it is possible by the vigorous practice of Pranayama and breathing regularly in a yogic way – attentive and deep.

**Brahman is responsible for everything**

Though MP is responsible for life, the truth is that the overall responsibility to keep the heart beating involuntarily lies with Brahman alone. MP along with Pancha Pranas, Pancha upa-Pranas, and Aham Prana form the energies of life. These Pranas are all demigods – semi-divine energies, which make things happen in the micro world. These Pranas and upa-Pranas are the instruments in the hands of MP, who uses them to perform various activities in the micro as well as macro worlds. However, MP himself is an instrument in the hands of Brahman, who uses him to perform all the actions of the Pranas. Let's look into the activities of Pranas in brief

## Pranas in the micro world

### Pancha Pranas

Following are the Pancha Pranas: - Prana, Apana, Vyana, Samana, and Udana

There are altogether 49 different kinds of Prana energies other than MP, working within the micro and macro worlds. The 11 include Pancha Pranas and Pancha upa-Pranas – Naga, Kurma, Krikala, Devadatta, and Dhananjaya. In a way, these Prana energies make the life complete in all the living beings. Let's see briefly what upa-Pranas do.

### Pancha Upa-Pranas

Following are the Pancha Upa-Pranas and their functionalities

- Naga: He regulates burping in us.
- Kurma: He controls closing, opening, and blinking of eyes.
- Krikala: He enables sneezing and coughing in us.
- Devadatta: He empowers us with the sensation of hunger and thirst, whenever our stomach is empty or whenever water content is less in the body or both. Whenever the body is short of oxygen, he makes us yawn so that extra oxygen can be taken in.
- Dhananjaya: He makes the heart valve open and close regularly

## Pranas in the macro world

The Pranas also called Vayus, play significant roles in the macro world. Consider our planet earth, we can see 37 Pranas at work from the surface, right up to the stratosphere and beyond, under the supervision and control of Pravaha Vayu. These 38 Pranas are toiling round-the-clock to maintain temperature and pressure differences so that the cloud formation and cloud movements happen at the appropriate time. This will result in monsoons, which in turn will lead to the harvesting of crops. The cultivated crop will sustain life on the planet earth.

## Sensory Organs and their deities

Sensory organs – eyes, nose, tongue, skin, and ears form the 5 windows to the external world through which external information enters the body and influence the mind.

Eyes see ears hear, tongue tastes, skin feels and nose smells but with the help of the mind. Without the involvement of the mind, the eyes cannot see, the nose cannot smell, the tongue cannot taste and the skin cannot feel.

## Manas is everything

Sensory organs have many demigods or semi energies supporting the activities. However, the demigods that control the mind are of foremost importance.

For example, when we are seeing something, if our mind is elsewhere, we won't be able to register in our minds, what we have seen and worst, we won't be able to remember it too.

## **Functions of Manas**

The Manas is everything because the image of the seen object gets in through the eyes and falls on the Manas. The intellect (Buddhi) picks up from there, processes it and compares it with the image in the Chitta (CM), to know if the seen object is known or unknown. If the object is known and if it is the image of a person, the intellect will attach the name and other information related to the person and passes it on to the Manas. This is how the Manas will recognize the person instantaneously.

Now, suppose when the eyes have seen an object – person, if the mind is not in sync with the eyes (that means, not being attentive), then the image doesn't fall on the Manas for further processing. Instead, the image falls on nothing, hence it is lost and this is exactly the reason why sometimes we fail to notice people (known or unknown to us) who smile or wave at us, even though we see them waving or smiling at us. This is because the Manas is elsewhere, deeply involved in thinking something.

Similarly, we won't be able to enjoy the food we eat, if Manas is busy with something - watching TV programs, reading a book, conversing with others, etc. In fact, we won't even be able to figure out what we are eating, if Manas is not with us, that is the power of the Mind.

Also, when we are talking, it is utmost important to have Manas focused on what we are saying or what we want to say. If in case the Manas is elsewhere while talking, we tend to talk nonsense and then repent later. This is true with other sensory organs also.

The controlling deities of the Manas are as follows:
- Prajanya – Kaksha 20
- Agni - Kaksha 15
- Chandra - Kaksha 12
- Indra - Kaksha 8
- Kama – Kaksha 8
- Paarvati – Kaksha 7
- Garuda – Kaksha 5
- Sesha – Kaksha 5
- Rudra – Kaksha 5
- Mukhya Prana – Kaksha 3
- Chaturmukha Brahma – Kaksha 3
- Lakshmi – Kaksha 2
- Narayana – Kaksha - 1

There are many deities behind every sensory organ. For example

The controlling deities of eyes (chakshus in Sanskrit) are
- Chandra (left) – Kaksha 12
- Surya (right) – Kaksha 12
- Syambhuva Manu (both) – Kaksha 10
- Bharathi – Kaksha 4
- Chaturmukha Brahma – Kaksha 3
- Narayana – Kaksha 1

Though the activities of the body look simple at the outset, they are seriously complex when we analyse. For example, we tend not to care much as to how our speech happens or we generally do not care to know the science behind our communication.

## The science behind our communication

The communication always begins in the Manas as thoughts are seeded there. For example: - If someone has to ask questions to the other like "Hello, how are you? May I know your name please?", these questions appear in the subtle form inside the Manas only as pure feelings. That means, the person feels like knowing how the other person is doing and what his name is. Feelings are just emotions so language is NOT attached to it just yet in the Mind. Let us look at the process.

- **Paraa stage**

    The feelings in the mind result in subtle vibrations near the naval – lower belly, where the Vaishvanara Agni– invisible divine energy in the form of fire is seated. Lord Krishna states in chapter 15 of Bhagavat Geeta: "Aham Vaishwanaro bhutwa Praninam dehamashritah. Pranapana samayukthah pachamyannam chaturvidham" – I, by being inside all the living beings as Vaishvanara Agni, make them breathe-in and breathe-out to keep them alive. Also, I am the one who digests their 4 different types of food they consume, to make them live healthily.

    That means, the food every living being consumes is further processed and digested by this Agni in its stomach and keeps the body warm. In case, if the body temperature is sub-optimal, then the person is said to be sick. Also, when the fire is extinguished, the body gets cold and the person is said to be dead. So, as long as the Agni maintains optimum body temperature, the person is said to be in good health. It is here at the seat of Vaishvanara Agni, the speech vibrations start. These vibrations are so subtle that they are neither heard nor felt. This stage of communication is called "Paraa".

- **Pashyanti**

    From the lower belly, they move up and the vibrations get grosser while reaching the heart. Now the vibrations can be felt and heard only by those who have inner ears to hear the sound. This stage of communication is called "Pashyanti".

- **Madhyama**

    The vibrations get further grosser and move up from the heart to the throat; it is where the vibrations are converted into communicative sentences. This stage of communication is called "Madhyama". At this stage, the sentences of the language (we intend to speak), are formed in our Manas and through the sound box near the throat, the sound is made. The sound is raw and appears to have no meaning; it is just a sound with vibrations.

- **Vaikhiri**

    The vibrations now get the grossest state and reach the mouth. It is here that the vibrations are converted into sound waves with a rhythm. With the help of opening and closing of lips, twisting and twirling of the tongue, the thoughts so aroused in the Manas get converted into audible sentences, spoken by the mouth in the language we intend to speak.

## The complexity of speech in a nutshell

It is the activities at Madhyama and Vaikhiri states, which are the most convoluted ones. The thoughts at the Madhyama stage are converted into sentences in the mind. The mind should know, how each of the words is pronounced in the language it is to be spoken. However, the complete data pertaining to the phonetics of the chosen language is stored in the Chitta (CM). The intellect (Buddhi) has to process the sentences in the Manas word-by-word by looking at the phonetics of the language from the CM. For each of the word in the sentences, the intellect picks up the equivalent phonetics from the CM and passes it to the mind. The complete sentences are now formed in the mind, in the subtle form of sound. Through the sound box near the throat, the Manas pushes the sound vibrations - the grossest of all, further up to the mouth. Now the sound vibrations have reached the stage of delivery. The sound vibrations need to be pronounced properly, in order to be understood by others and that's when the communication is said to be complete. That is done through the synchronous movements of the tongue and lips. The sound versions of punctuations, full stops, commas, semicolons, etc. are added in the sentences before we speak and the tongue and lip movements have to incorporate that.

This complex activity happens without our conscious attempt and knowledge. That means, things happen on their own and we don't have to be scientists, philosophers, speech therapists or other intelligent people to speak. Anyone can speak the language he is fluent in and that's the beauty of it. Also, this explains how Manas plays a significant role in the speech.

## Thoughts are complicated too

The similar kind of complex activities happen even when we are thinking or worrying about something. It is just that, the sound vibration won't be delivered as speech through the mouth but the intensity of churning inside the Manas, Buddhi, and Chitta is the same.

# Everything depends on Brahman for existence

### Is Brahman that indispensable to the Universe?

To answer this question, lets first consider our body and list out a few of the multi-million activities happen inside, to determine if we have any control over them.

Man is in one of the three states

Man goes through 3 states on a daily basis and they are Sleeping, walking and dreaming.

- **Sleeping**

    We lie on the bed, close our eyes and do not know what happens next. We are not sure when and how we fell asleep. Why do we get into deep sleep sometimes? Why is our sleep disturbed some other times? – We don't know. What took us to sleep and what brought us out of sleep? - We don't know. Also, we wake up from sleep, sometimes restful and sometimes not that restful, why? - We have no right answer to these queries. But the truth is, we hardly know anything about sleep as it remains a deep mystery to us. We sleep because we feel sleepy and wakeup because we are woken up. But one thing is true, we all experience bliss in deep sleep. The reason as per "Manduka Upanishad", -Vishnu being at the Anahata chakra (Heart chakra – a vortex of energy) induces sleep to the Aatma. The Vedanta says, man is blissful in deep sleep because he is in communion with the infinitely blissful GOD – Narayana.

There are some ways to adapt to this sleep pattern. "Yoga Nidra" – the yogic way of sleeping, is one of them. However, it teaches how to adapt to sleep, not the mastery and control of sleep itself. This shows how vulnerable we are to sleep as we experience sleep daily but we don't know what exactly it is. It is so very strange.

- **Waking**

    In the waking state, our Indriyas (sensory organs), Aatma, Manas, Intellect, and Chitta (mind) get activated. We get attentive and are ready physically, emotionally and mentally to begin the daily activities. As long as the above-described organs are activated and remain in coordination with each other, we seem to be awake and attentive to all the events happening around us. But unfortunately, in the waking state, the mind will get back the awareness and thoughts like "I", "Me", "Mine", "Myself", etc. which is the root cause of our anxiety, fear, worries, sadness, etc.

These thoughts were absent when we were in deep sleep so we were blissful. This is so because before going to sleep, we mentally handed-over the responsibility of our families and ourselves into the hands of the divine like an innocent child and we slept carefreely. So, we were blissful. However, we don't do it consciously though.

When we wake up, we notice that everything seems to have been well taken care of as nothing is in disarray during our sleep. So we are happy for that but that happiness is short-lived, the moment we take back our responsibilities from the hands of the divine onto our shoulders. So as usual, worries will begin at that moment itself.

However, Manduka Upanishad states that, Vishnu switches-on and activates the Ajna chakra (Brow chakra), while de-activating or switching off the Anahata chakra. The Vedanta states, the man experiences "false ego", "anxiety", "worries" and "depression" because the centre of activity shifts away from the heart - the seat of Vishnu and Aatma, to the space between the eyebrows - the centre for "logic", "intellect", "ego", etc., the home of all the troubles. If the Ajna chakra is not charged through meditation, our egos/ arrogance/ anger, etc. will drive us leading to troubles in life.

However, there is a big philosophy hidden behind our sleep, which we all should understand and learn from that, says the Vedanta. Again, the waking up state is totally not in our control too.

- **Dreaming**

    We all get dreams regularly and the dream state is one of the 3 states (sleeping, waking & dreaming) we live in. In the deep sleep state, all the above-mentioned organs are rested. So, there is absolutely no mental activity. In waking state, all organs are active and the person is mentally and physically equipped for the daily grind. However, in the dream state, all except Manas and Chitta are partially active.

    Manduka Upanishad states that Vishnu switches off both Ajna and Anahata chakras and activates Vishuddhi chakra, near the throat. That's when we start viewing dreams through our Manas. The Manas has the ability to see, feel smell and sense, which the blind people use it for navigating on the streets. When the external eyes are blocked, Manas based eyes are opened to see things around.

    We get to view our dreams on a small screen whose size is just a space as small as the tip of the needle, which is present on the "epiglottis", just above the throat. On a screen that is of the size of a dot, we get to see the world in our dream state.

What dream we get to see is absolutely not in our discretion though. Whatever is projected on that small screen, we have to watch and that's it. Sometimes it is pleasant, some other times it could be a nightmarish one, which we watch with fright and sweat but all these in the dream state.

So once again, we have no control over this state too, as whatever is being shown in the dream, we have to see without any control over it.

Other activities humans involuntarily perform

- **<u>Seeing</u>**

    We are born with eyes and by 3 months of our existence on the earth, we start seeing the objects around and by 6 months we start to recognize them and by 12 we learn the art of seeing, observing, recognizing and even passing gestures vocally. We are seeing because we have eyes, that's it. We have done nothing to earn our eyesight. You don't have to be rich or famous or privileged to have eyes and see. The divine has blessed us with eyes irrespective of who we are. The sad part is, we don't take a moment to understand what goes behind our seeing as we take it for granted without expressing our gratitude to the divine.

The seeing activity entails complex sub-activities, which involves eyes, Manas, Buddhi (intellect) and Chitta (conscious memory). The onus of bringing all these organs in line and coordinate with each other lies squarely with the unseen subtle energies acting overtime behind our seeing. The moment one or more energies give up our eyes will malfunction. Our vision may get myopic and we may lose eyesight permanently.

We are in no way equipped to stop the degradation of eyesight as we don't own and control our vision.

- **Eating**

    Eating is another complex activity, which involves tooth to chew, tongue to taste and enjoy the food. Also, salivary glands to salivate and mix the ground-food compounds with saliva – a digestive enzyme and finally, swallow by pushing it down the throat, into the stomach. If the energy – "Varuna" responsible for the functioning of salivary glands is not active or mildly active, then the saliva is either not secreted or not abundantly secreted. That's when chewing and swallowing food will be a herculean task. It may result even in death at times due to the choking of the throat. Saliva is that crucial for eating whose secretion is not in our control.

Taking food down the throat into the stomach is the work of "Apana" energy. Eating implies sending nutrition into the body for keeping it hale and healthy. However, to bring the food into the mouth, the hand has to do the job. It is so strange, even in the darkest of the dark places, our hands can always reach our mouths, without any confusion.

Also, when we are eating, say for example a masala dosa, while chewing the dosa, the tongue grasps the taste, the intellect (Buddhi) parallelly processes the taste information and compares it with the data in the Chitta. That's when we come to know if the dosa made is better than the earlier one OR not appealing enough OR tastes foul not like a regular dosa. The processing work happens with every bite and every time we chew it.

To see the food on the plate, the eyes have to work. So, all connected organs for both hands and eyes have to work with organs related to eating. They can only work in harmony if and only if all the demigods work together with utmost co-ordination. This illustration shows eating too is not in our control as we sometimes overeat in hurry and suffer relaxedly. We end up with indigestion and bloated feelings because of that.

- **Breathing**

    Human life is anchored on 11 different Pranas (wind currents) with Mukhya Prana (MP) supervising and tightly controlling them. They in turn control human life.

    When we die, MP along with 11 Pranas (5 Pancha Pranas and 5 Pancha upa-Pranas plus Aham Prana) leave our body and then Aatma departs from the body along with all other remaining energies.

    So, as long as MP is inside the body, all other Pranas also stay inside. Hence, other energies too will remain intact inside the body, as a result, the person is deemed to be alive. He may be sick and diseased but he will still be alive because Pranas are present in his body. We may have a high opinion about ourselves and about our capabilities, as we tend to over-estimate ourselves often. But the truth is that the very essence of our living – life, is not in our control, what an irony!!.

- **Working**

    We all perform activities on a day-to-day basis at offices, business establishments, institutions, etc. During our work, all the sensory organs – eyes, nose, ears, tongue, and skin get active. Along with them, Manas, Buddhi, Chitta, mouth, hands, and legs also get active. Mouth is used for communicating with others.

Let us consider, for example, the work of writing a piece of software, which sits on the mobile tower to enable the mobile connectivity. To write the software code, one uses Buddhi, Manas, Chitta, hands, and eyes. To communicate, one uses the mouth; to hear others' view, he uses ears and to move around he uses his legs to walk.

The demigods, who control the hands, are as follows:
- Daksha Prajapati – Kaksha 10
- Indra – Kaksha 8

**Various activities, which happen behind our work:**

The desire to do any work is seeded in the Manas first, which is moved to the Buddhi (intellect) for processing. The Buddhi, in turn, will pass on the instructions to do the Manas as to how to do the work. The Manas will move the hands to perform the activity. Any activity - writing, typing, drawing, sculpting, carving, painting, etc. can only be performed, if the information to perform is there in the Manas. For example, a painter will first have the image of the picture in his mind. The Buddhi processes it and provides the information as to how to go about painting it. Now all he has to do is paint using his hands, which requires absolute co-ordination between his mind and the hand. Daksha and Indra – the demigods of hands establish this co-ordination seamlessly and with the demigods of the mind, make the painting activity happen.

Also, we walk, run and jump around easily without thinking much. The demigods which help us do all these are as follows:

- Jayanta (Eternal son of Indra) – Kaksha 19
- Samba (Eternal son of Indra) – Kaksha 19

For doing a simple work, we feel astonished when we know the sheer number of energies at play behind the scene. Anyone energy not fully active means, we deliver sub-standard work. In such a scenario, how can we claim, "I did the job"? How silly is to make such a false claim?

In fact, the credit should go to the demigods for doing the work through us. We are instruments in their hands and they, in turn, are the instruments in the hands of Narayana.

So, every activity happening within our body has many energies working behind the scene, without even giving us any clue about it. The selfless services of these energies make us who we are, so we need to acknowledge that. The truth that comes to the limelight is, we are puppets in the hands of the demigods as they make us dance to their tunes. They seed the thoughts through emotions in our minds and make us perform activities as reactions to those emotions. They do it like puppeteers controlling the puppets.

Without knowing this truth, we think we are the doers of the Karmas (activities). This is the root of all our problems as doing that means, taking the ownership of the Karmas, which were performed using us. However, the ownership comes with the fruits of Karmas – Good OR Bad. Taking the ownership of Karma means accepting the fruits of it too, which bind us to Karma. Our Karmas push us into the jaws of the horrifying cycle of birth & death, which comes with never-ending agonies.

However, taking the ownership of the Karmas is like a knife taking the responsibility for killing someone and scissors taking the ownership for the success of the operation, performed on the patient by a doctor. The truth is, the credit or blame should go to the doctor alone who used the scissors and other instruments to operate.

### **Do demigods perform all our actions?**

The demigods are not independent either, as they are also not the real doers. We have seen earlier that one who has the complete ownership and the control of all the aspects of Karma, is the real doer of the same. For that to happen, one has to be independent, not dependent on other forces for existence. However, the demigods are not independent so they are not the real doers.

The way we are the instruments in the hands of demigods, who are at the lower Kakshas, these demigods are also the instruments in the hands of those at the higher Kakshas. The forces of the higher Kakshas are, however, the instruments in the hands of Brahman.

This means to say, the Brahman is the ultimate doer of everything through the demigods across the micro and macro worlds.

## Why demigods have to depend on Brahman?

Saint Madhvacharya in his works has stated that there are only 2 entities in the Universe - the independent and dependent entities.

Since the demigods belong to the other group (dependent entities), they have to depend on Narayana for their very existence as beings. Nothing can exist, move, perform, think, communicate, so on and so forth on its own other than Narayana. Only HE has the abilities to do everything independently. So, HE only can bring activities in the demigods through the Universal principle "Subtle moves the gross". That's the reason, why the demigods depend on Narayana to perform their activities.

## How powerful is Brahman?

Vedas narrate an incident happened several millennia (over 10,000 years) ago, during Vedic times at a school deep inside a forest. A student asks his Guru (teacher) as to how powerful is the Brahman, who is also called GOD. The Guru closed his eyes, took a deep breath and started making uncomfortable facial gestures. This was because it was a difficult question to answer for him as one can only experience GOD, which cannot be understood through explanation. However, explaining his inner experience through words was a challenge for him, yet he couldn't ignore the question because the student would be disappointed. Later, he beautifully narrates his inner experience like this.

*"When I was meditating with the closed eyes, I had a vision of the divine feet of Lord Narayana. Under the tiny toe of HIS feet, I saw a brilliantly shining dust particle. Upon analysis, I discovered that it is the infinitely vast, expansive Universe in which we live. This tells how powerful GOD is; even the Universe is just like a dust particle in front of HIM. HE is that powerful".*

## The Universe is NOT infinite but the space in which it is seated is

Another important observation about the Universe made by the risihis thorough their deep contemplation and meditation is that the Universe is finite but the empty space (avyaktha aakasha in Sanskrit) in which the Universe is located is infinite.

When compared to the infinite avyaktha aakasha, the Universe, whose length, width and depth are measured in billions of light years, is not even a spec. However, Brahman has occupied entire avyaktha aakasha by not even sparing an inch of it. Now one can to some extent imagine how big and powerful GOD is.

## Definition of "Bhagvan" – the most revered title for GOD

The Holy Scriptures like "Vishnu Purana (VP)" – written over 5000 years ago by sage Vyasa, declares that only Lord Narayana is addressed as "Bhagvan". This is due to the fact that only HE has all the 6 qualities required to bag the coveted title "Bhagvan".

The six qualities are described in the verses as follows.

"*aiśvaryasya samagrasya*

*vīryasya yaśasaḥ śriyaḥ*

*jñāna-vairāgyayoś caiva*

*ṣaṇṇāṁ bhagam itīṅganā*". Its meaning is as follows.

- **Aishwarya (Absolute ownership of everything)**

    One should have the ownership of every inch of space in the material and subtle Universe. So, everything that exists in the material and subtle worlds should belong to him. However, mere ownership of everything won't be sufficed to earn this title, there should be a total lordship over everything. That means, he should have out-and-out control over everything in these worlds. Also, one who can make the Universe dance to his tunes and for whom the Universal creation, sustenance, and annihilation is just a child's play, qualifies to be called Bhagvan.

- **Virya (Unparalleled Courage OR Valor)**

    One, who has the courage and ability to bring down and annihilate every kind of opposition to the Universal order of the divine, is called Bhagvan. Vedanta describes, "veer" and "shoor" as twin words. Veer is the inner strength – physical and mental, required to win over the opponents. Shoor is the outer expression of the same. So, one who has the immense inner strength and is capable to exhibit it externally, to maintain the Universal law-and-order can be qualified as Bhagvan.

- **Yashas (loosely translated as Fame)**

    One who is widely known and is very famous among all the living beings, including demigods, across the material and spiritual worlds qualify to be addressed as Bhagvan.

- **Shri (Opulence)**

Vedanta talks about 8 qualities, which represent Shri. They are as follows:

- Gaja (loosely translated as royalty),
- Santana (loosely translated as parenthood),
- Veer (inner strength/ valor),
- Vijay (victory),
- Dhaanya (loosely translated as good harvest),

- <u>Aishwarya</u> (lordship),
- <u>Dhana</u> (loosely translated as affluence),

- **<u>Adhrushta</u>** (loosely translated as good luck OR fortune).

    Lakshmi, who controls the "Shri" is also the granter of the same to the individuals (Aatmas) based on their past Karmas. However, she, in turn, is under the direct control of Lord Narayana, as HE pulls the strings to make her grant Shri to the individuals based on their past Karmas. So, the one who controls Lakshmi who in turn controls Shri qualifies to be addressed as Bhagvan.

- **<u>Jnana (knowledge)</u>**

    One who has the complete knowledge (infinite in width and depth) of everything, which exists in the material as well as the subtle Universe, qualifies to be called as Bhagvan.

- **<u>Vairagya (Complete renouncement)</u>**

    One who has the sense of absolute renouncement despite being the richest and the most powerful in the Universe. Also, the one, who is selfless to the core and performs every action selflessly, qualifies to be addressed as Bhagvan.

Since only Lord Narayana OR Brahman has all these six qualities to the fullest extent, HE is the real Bhagvan OR GOD OR Lord of the Universe.

Let us understand the concept of "subtle moves the gross" in order to know how Brahman, being infinitely subtle, performs all the Universal activities through grosser demigods.

# Subtle moves the gross

**Subtle mind moves the gross body**

We have seen in the earlier chapters how our mind, which is subtle in nature makes us physically do things in our day-to-day lives. If our body has to move, the mind has to direct it. This is what is termed "Subtle moving the gross".

For example, if a desire to go for a stroll is seeded in our mind, then we just wear the walking gear and head out straight for walking. While walking if a desire to drink a cappuccino coffee is developed in the mind, we will end up in any coffee shop within no time to sip coffee. Similarly, the mind decides what we have to say while we are conversing with others. We have seen this too in the earlier chapters. Our anger first seeded in our mind in the form of emotions and this (emotion) makes us shout at others and get into the physical duel with them if the situation deteriorates further.

So, our mind being much subtler than our gross body, it makes us dance to its tunes. However, our mind also is not independent. It takes orders from the demigods, who are much subtler than our mind. They (demigods) instill the desires in our mind, which in turn make us dance to the tunes of demigods. This is to say, the

demigods drive us through our mind. But the truth is, they too are not independent either. They take orders from much subtler forces on the higher Kakshas, who in turn are driven by the forces higher up on the Kakshas. Finally, the subtlest of all the subtle forces,
the infinitely subtle force – Narayana drives everything in Universe. That means, as per our past Karmas, it is HIM who makes us dance to HIS tunes through the demigods. Let us see what Vedanta says about it

## What does Vedanta say about the doership?

Vedanta refers Brahman as "Vishwa Karmah", "Vishwa Chakshus", "Vishwa Karnah", "Mahashanh", "Vishwa Saakshih", "Vishwa Shilpih" and the like. We have read in the last few chapters that there are various demigods and black energies which influence living beings in general and humans in particular.

### Vishwa Karmah

The word "Vishwa Karmah" indicates that every activity in the Universe – micro and macro worlds is performed by the Brahman. To understand the gravity of this statement, let's consider the human body in the micro world, which has billions of cells. Each cell plays its role to keep the body intact. It is to be known that the cells do age, as they too have a lifespan. At the end of the lifespan, cells die only to be replaced with newly born cells. Therefore, at any given time, there is a constant death and birth of cells happening seamlessly in the body.

This means cellular level activities alone is billion plus in number. Now think of the labor required to make the sensory and all other organs, including the functioning of heart and lungs, plus the exercises done to make us execute our day-to-day duties. All of this will add up to several billion actions being carried out from the womb to tomb, 24x7 and 365 days. Keeping one human body alive and kicking entails this unexplainable amount of hard labor. Now imagine what it is like doing it, in every individual human body throughout the world. It is estimated that there are over 6 billion people living on this planet.

<u>Are the activities relegated to humans alone?</u> – NO, there are birds, fishes, animals, worms, insects and every other living being on the planet. Who will do the tasks inside their bodies? - Brahman and no wonder why HE is called "Vishwa Karmah" – the Universal scale performer of tasks.

## <u>Vishwa Chakshus</u>

One, who by residing in every living being sees everything and decides what is to be shown to the living being is called Vishwa Chakshus. We all know that demigods are behind seeing in every living being in general and humans in particular. The demigods Surya and Chandra are the energies behind seeing in humans. So they are subtler than us, they see more than what we see; however, the Brahman being in them (demigods) and subtlest of all, will see more than what the demigods see. In fact, in the Universe, nothing can be hidden from him. HE alone has a 360-degree view of the entire Universe. So, he is Vishwa Chakshus, the Universal observer.

Why is there filtering, why not show everything? – We have no hold on seeing. What is shown, we will have to see. Suppose if someone has to trip and fall to break his backbone as a punishment for his wrongdoings in his past life, the demigods won't show him the banana peel lying on the path, they either make him look elsewhere or make him un-attentive by keeping his mind engrossed on something else while walking. The demigods of eyes will co-ordinate with the demigods of legs (Jayanta and Samba are the demigods for enabling movements) to make the person step on the banana peel, skid, fall and break his backbone.

Will demigods have the list of all the wrongdoings and punishments of everyone? – No, only Brahman has it. When the time comes, HE will pull the strings on them (demigods), they, in turn, pull the strings on us. We are puppets in the hands of demigods and they are puppets in the hands of Brahman, that's it. So, no one has the freedom to do what he or she wants, all have to do what Brahman wants. In fact, HE will make us do things using the demigods, which is the secret only through deep contemplation that one can understand. Whenever, whatever has to happen will happen, no matter how much we try to stop it.

## Vishwa Karnah

One who resides in the ears of all living being and makes them hear what they should and block the rest is called Vishwa Karnah. HE is none other than Brahman. HE listens and understands the communication of every living being – be it reptiles, worms, insects, bugs, amphibians, fishes, birds, animals and humans on the planet earth.

We have seen that hearing in humans is enabled by the demigods (Chandra and dighdevatas) and they decide what one should hear and how much. Let's analyze this in bit detail; as a boon for the good deeds done in the past life, let's consider a student in the classroom is destined to score high marks in the exam and get admiration from everyone. The two semi-divine energies make him listen clearly to the lecture, without any distortion. They do so by coordinating with demigods of Manas, eyes, Buddhi and Chitta to make the student be attentive in the class, decipher the lecture well and store it in the Chitta (memory) for later recalls. This is how the student listens, understands and remembers what he heard.

The demigods play important roles inside the student's body in order to keep him attentive in the class. However, the truth is, they are not doing it independently but are being driven to do things by the Brahman himself. This is so because the demigods are subtler than the student and the Brahman is infinitely subtler than them. Always subtle moves the gross – a Universal principle.

In humans, Brahman also called Narayana can listen to the spoken and non-spoken words. HE is the only divine who can comprehend our inner non-communicative feelings, our pains, our emotions, etc. One who understands this will fall in love with the divine forever.

## Mahashanh

HE is the one who resides inside every living being and eats every food consumed by him. HE decides as to what a living being should eat and how much. By residing inside, HE makes sure the creature is well fed to live till he (the living being) dies.

Being infinitely subtle and inside every living being, the Brahman consumes every kind of food these living creatures eat. HE eats and makes the creature eat too; that's why he is called Mahashanh, a Universal eater.

HE is the one who determines what food one has to eat. If HE decides that an individual should have a sumptuous dinner, he (the individual) will get an unexpected invitation for a celebration cum dinner. We have seen that happening in our lives too.

If due to some karmic reasons in the past life, an individual is supposed to struggle very hard for even a simple meal, the Brahman sitting inside, makes sure it happens. HE (Brahman) uses other demigods to set the environment so that earning money becomes extremely difficult for the individual. With all the toil, he will hardly earn any money to survive, despite having all the skills. So, having a simple meal once a day will be a big deal for the person, thus making him shed tears looking at his own plight. Mahashanh makes an individual experience the pain in life, what he gave to others in his past.

## Vishwa Shilpih

When we look at nature, her beauty will mesmerize us; the sheer variety of objects is really breathtaking. We also wonder how the creator created nature so elegantly, who can inspire everyone. However, there are few people, mostly intellectuals who deny the existence of any creator. Their argument is, nature evolved on its own over a period of time. So no creator is required. Their statement makes no sense because the same people when they visit any museum, they admire the art works on display and ask the curator as to who is the artist of so and so art. There, they never accept the argument that there was no artist behind the art and that it evolved on its own over a period of time.

The point to ponder is when a simple work of art had to have an artist, why, not the infinitely complex nature? Why not the expansive Universe?

Vedanta says the creator of this Universe is Brahman. There is uniqueness in HIS creation, meaning, no two materials are the same. This is very interesting, let alone two persons born out of the same womb not being the exactly similar. Even two fruits or flowers of the same plant or tree are not the same taste or appearance and fragrance. There are minute differences, which can only be spotted through the microscope. Our eyes, nose, and tongue have no power to make out those minute differences. Also, two leaves of the same tree or plant have 100% similarity, there are variations. In a nutshell, everything in the Universe is unique.

The Universe was in the ionic state – in the form of atoms and electrons widely spread across before the creation activity started, as nothing was in solid form then.

The way kids create various objects out of clay, the Brahman created various objects out of a heap of ions – the Universe in the primordial state. We use wheat flour to make various eatables of various shapes and sizes through different methods of cooking; likewise, the Brahman also makes several Universal objects out of pure ions.

He created gigantic stars, asteroids, milky ways, our solar system, the sun and the nine planets and their satellites, etc. He gave shape to every living creatures, hills, trees, shrubs, fruits, mountains, rivers, oceans, seas, etc. by being inside them, just like we do injection blow molding for making plastic containers.

<u>Why is an elephant like what he is?</u> – The answer is, the infinitely subtle Brahman is inside an elephant in the form of an elephant, giving shape to it.

Why is a rose flower so beautiful? Why does it have a pleasing fragrance? – It is so because the Brahman is inside the rose in the form of a rose, giving shape and aroma to it.

If a woman is beautiful, HE is inside her as a beautiful woman and so He is inside a man as a man. In fact, the femininity of a female and masculinity of a male is HIS (Brahman's) contribution.

Since HE is the essence of everything, the nature of an object is because of HIM. That means, the rosiness of rose flower which makes a rose a rose, the mangoness of a mango fruit which makes a mango a mango, is because of HIM. Vishwa Shilpih, by being inside everything in the Universe, gives its shape, size and contributes to its nature.

## **The sound byte of every language is the epithet of Brahman**

There are emotions behind the communication of all living beings, including humans. The communication is the expression of our emotions through rhythm, which is also called the accent of our speech (communication). People understand what we say only through our accent. Likewise, every living being, be it animals, worms, insects, birds, apes, reptiles, amphibians express their emotions to others of the same species through their unique accent.

## Let us understand who each of the sound made by living beings refers to

Whenever we feel (emotions) like calling someone, we say in English "Hey, come here". The emotions inside our mind to call someone towards us to come out through our speech. Whom are we addressing this through communication? -

When we call someone saying, "Hey, come here", we are addressing the real indweller of that body. That is the owner of the body.

Who is the owner of the body? – Vedanta claims that Brahman is the true owner of the body of all the living beings. Aatma is attached helplessly inside the body since he has no control over anything in the body. So, whoever has the ownership of the whole body, is the controller of the body. Hence the body belongs to Brahman. In the truest sense, the statement, "Hey, come here" is to call Brahman, not the Aatma. The Aatma of the person will accompany wherever GOD takes, that's it.

This is true with every language used for communication. Every living being – animals, birds, reptiles, worms, bugs, etc. express their feelings through their mode of communication. In essence, they too are pointing at GOD because the essence of everything within the Universe and outside is Brahman only.

He is inside mountains in the form of mountains, inside trees in the form of trees, inside flowers in the form of flowers, inside clouds in the form of clouds, inside rivers in the form of rivers, inside birds in the form of birds, inside rice in the form of rice, inside corn in the form of corn and the list goes on and on and is infinite.

So, all the sounds made by nature – thunder sound of lightning, the sound of rains, the sound of waterfalls, the sound of sea waves, the sound of rustling leaves, the sound of the wind, the buzzing sound of bees, the chirping of birds and also the fragrance of the flowers, the sweetness of fruits, the taste of rice and corn, all reveal GOD only.

This is because, HE being the essence of everything, gives every object its character. That means HE makes an apple fruit taste like an apple, as tasting like an apple is the GUNA or nature of the apple fruit. An apple cannot taste like a banana, which is against its GUNA. This is how he brings out the uniqueness of every object.

### Let's understand "subtle moves the gross" in detail.

Vedas refer to the Brahman as what has been stated above, but in reality, HE is infinitely much more than that. However, when we observe in detail, we notice the constant meddling or interfering of demigods in the human life. Why is it so?

The reality is that the gross has no ability to perform any action on its own, only subtle can induce it in the gross. If we consider the human body, it is always the mind that moves the body, it is so because the mind is subtler than the body. However, the mind is moved by the emotions and thoughts, which are seeded by the sensory organs. Since they (emotions) are subtler than the mind, they move the mind. Always, the mind takes the orders from the emotions and the gross body takes orders from the mind. So, in a nutshell, emotions move the mind and mind moves the gross body. Let us understand this statement in detail.

Example: -

When we hear about the super hit movie "Bahubali 2 – the ending" and view the film promotional videos on the YouTube, we are caught in the web of temptations to watch the movie. The temptations are induced in the mind by the emotions, which in turn are induced by the eyes and ears. Constant hearing and watching the promotional videos of the movie turn temptations into cravings, which will give rise to thoughts and the determination in the mind, to somehow watch the movie at all cost. So, even if the tickets are not available, we end up watching the movie, paying "marked-up" price for the same. This is how, the sensory organs move the mind through emotions, which in turn moves the body.

The emotions and thoughts introduced by the sensory organs are subtler than the mind. Intellect (Buddhi) is even subtler. The Chitta

& Chetana (Conscious & sub-conscious minds) is much subtler than the Intellect.

Nevertheless, to make the human body dance to its tunes, the mind should be intelligent, being subtle is not enough. But the mind is insentient and dumb but then what makes the mind do intelligent things? – The answer is demigods. They, being subtler than the mind, bring the required intelligence not only to the mind but also to the other organs in the human body. They (all organs) also make the body dance to their tunes, using the mind. So the mind is intermediary for everything. When the mind is dead during deep sleep, we will never experience pain at all.

To understand the intelligence a bit more in detail, let's take the example of a smartphone. Though the smartphone is dumb, what makes it smart? The software app on it makes it smart. You can use the phone to make audio/ video calls, browse the Internet, play games, etc. This explains the importance of being smart and intelligent.

## **Are all subtle energies really intelligent?**

No, only energy that is absolutely independent can be super intelligent and smart, so it's only Brahman who will fit the bill.

### Is Brahman responsible for the intelligence in the demigods?

Yes. However, Brahman uses demigods at the higher Kakshas, who are much more subtler and powerful, to control demigods at the lower Kakshas, who are much less powerful than those at the higher Kakshas. So, the demigods at the lower Kakshas draw intelligence from those at the higher Kakshas. Let's draw an analogy like this: If A controls B, B controls C, C controls D, D controls E, then A controls E.

### Do demigods have bodies like us?

They do have bodies like us and live in the celestial world. One of the demi-gods is Indra, who is the king of all the demigods and rules them at "Indra Loka" – the kingdom of demigods – a celestial world. His body also has Pancha koshas – 5 sheaths like (a) Annamaya (b) Pranamaya (c) Manomaya (d) Vijnana Maya (e) Anandamaya koshas. We have various demigods energizing these koshas. For Manas, we have Prajanya (Kaksha 20), Agni (Kaksha 15), Chandra (Kaksha 12), Indra (Kaksha 8) and others.

The celestial body of Prajanya has Manas too. However, Agni, Chandra, Indra and others at the higher Kakshas control his Manas. Similarly, the Manas in the celestial body of Agni is energized by Chandra, Indra, and other higher energies. Indra and higher energies control the Manas of Chandra. Indra's Manas is always controlled by only higher energies Garuda (Kaksha 5), Sesha

(Kaksha 5), Rudra (Kaksha 5), Bharathi Devi (Kaksha 4), Chaturmukha Brahma (Kaksha 3), Lakshmi (Kaksha 2) and Narayana (Kaksha 1).

That means energies of the lower Kakshas will never-ever be able to control or influence the energies at higher Kakshas. It's only one way, from higher to the lower.

## Why should these energies carry out the exercises mentioned above?

Everyone has two duties to perform. One is a personal duty and other is a societal duty.

Five thousand years ago, to make Arjuna perform his societal duties, Lord Krishna narrated Bhagavad Geeta to Arjuna, to instill the sense of duty and made him fight for the cause of reestablishing Dharma - righteousness, in the society. Arjuna had to fight against everyone – friends, relatives, and strangers, who stood against establishing Dharma in the world. Fighting the war was Arjuna's societal responsibility so Krishna made him do it by force.

So, the demigods also have social responsibilities and the Almighty GOD gave detailed responsibilities to all of them at various Kakshas. So, they do their duty that's all. In fact, duty is loosely translated as Karma in Sanskrit.

Let's throw some light on "Karma Theory".

# Nishkaama Karma – an analysis

### Nishkaama Karma (NK) in brief

Lord Krishna while reciting Bhagavad Geeta to Arjuna, recommends the mankind to perform every Karma (action in Sanskrit) as "Nishkaama Karma (NK)" – expectation-less action to achieve material and spiritual excellence in life. He means to say, every action - from household chores to mundane office works, from works that benefit the self to those that benefit the society, be performed with utmost devotion, dedication, and sincerity as a service to GOD. Performing all our actions this way will eventually result in invoking the divine consciousness in us. That means, we start getting divine qualities, which in turn will facilitate our escape from the cycle of birth-and-death one day and embrace Moksha (liberation in English) in the end. So, seeing every work as GOD's work or seeing GOD in every work is the key to liberation.

### Complexities involved in bringing NK to life

We have understood that any action performed detachedly leads to NK. However, it is not that simple as it sounds because many times though we perform actions detachedly, we do not accept the outcome of the work detachedly. It is to be noted that working detachedly is achievable but accepting the fruits of our toil detachedly is very difficult.

We always have expectations of the works we do. We may not say it loudly but in reality, we have expectations, deeply hidden in our hearts. It is this expectation that brings pain to us. We feel disappointed when the fruits of our work do not match with our anticipation. An action performed this way doesn't qualify to be called NK. Let us analyze the term expectation:

- **Expectations**

    We all have a whole lot of expectations from life. Some want to be rich and famous; some want to be successful in their careers. Some want to prosper as singers, actors, businessmen, scientists, etc. To put it simply, everyone expects happiness in life and man will put efforts to somehow get it. So, his day-to-day activities are in line with it but the question is with the definition of happiness. Man identifies pleasure, which is temporary in nature, with happiness and pursues it all his life. However, the pleasure is gross because the sensory organs, which induce it, are gross in nature. In contrast, happiness or bliss is much subtler and is deep and hence it lasts long. Let's come back to the discussion about the expectations.

## Why our efforts often do not fetch anticipated returns?

We get shattered, disappointed and sometimes feel suicidal when the results of our work doesn't bring anticipated returns. This is because our emotions are the byproduct of the attachment to the fruits of our actions. We always expect something in return as "bakshish" or reward for the work we have done. So, when we don't get it, we get mad. It is this that I was talking about earlier, which one should give up. The detached execution of a work is not enough but we should also have the magnanimity to accept the fruits of work, detachedly too.

There is a complicated philosophy hidden behind the Karma or the work we do. One should understand the philosophy when performing actions. Karma has two components:

- Our effort

    Effort - both physical and mental, required to do any work is our contribution. What is required from our side, we have to give it 100%. That means, we have to enthusiastically put efforts as if there is no tomorrow to complete the work.

- GOD's grace.

    GOD's grace is also termed as luck, which is equally important for the successful completion of any work and reap the returns. Whenever there is a shortfall in either our efforts OR luck OR both, work either fails to get completed OR if at all completed, doesn't bring the results as expected.

GOD's grace will only happen if the person deserves it. Even if he deserves it, the grace will happen only at the right time. We have seen that in the earlier chapters that everything in the Universe is time bound. Till the right time doesn't arrive, no event will happen and it is also applicable to GOD's grace. If we deserve something, we will get it at the appropriate time. However, we don't have the right to demand GOD's grace, as it is linked to our past Karmas It is only the divine which knows clearly who deserves what.

When we don't deserve something due to our past bad deeds, then our efforts to get it will go nowhere. No matter how much we struggle we fail to bring it in our life because of the past baggage. In such cases, we should accept the fact sportingly and move on.

## **Develop the sense of equanimity**

By being in the constant awareness that "I am not the doer but he is" will eventually make us detach from the outcome of the work, which will one day raise our consciousness towards the divine. That's when we rise above the dualities like "good and bad", "success and failure", "heat and cold", "pain and pleasure", "respect and insult", so on and so forth. That means, we develop the equanimity in life and remain blissful throughout. A person who has reached that stage is called "Sthitha Prajna (SP)". Nothing can ever make an SP sad, as he is always joyful. This is the stage Lord Krishna harps on in Bhagavad Geeta that one should achieve to reach HIM (the Lord).

### How to develop the feeling of non-doership all the time?

We know that Narayana or Brahman is inside everything giving shape and size to all the objects. Being infinitely subtle, HE is inside us also making the gross (us) dance to HIS (subtlest) tunes. HE is subtler than all the subtle things put together so HE literally brings activities in every object in the Universe. That means, HE makes everything move and that's the reality.

### The concept of object and its mirror image:

The 11th-century saint Madhvacharya in his works described the relationship between the Paramatma (Narayana) and Aatma or the relation between the infinite and the finite, which is just like the relationship between the object and its mirror image. He coined the term "Bimba Prati-Bimba" – Object and it's mirror image while explaining this beautiful relationship.

If the real object smiles, its mirror image smiles too. If the real object cries, its mirror image cries too. If the real object moves, the mirror image also moves. If the real object performs some actions, its mirror image performs actions too. If the real object eats, its mirror image eats too. If the real object speaks, its mirror image speaks too. In fact, Vedanta claims Narayana is the real speaker; HE uses humans as loudspeakers (instrument) only. In reality, HE speaks through our vocal chords using the demigods also as instruments.

The list goes on and on like this. So, in a way, the mirror image's existence itself depends on the real object. That means, if the real object goes off the mirror, there would be no mirror image and that's it.

This logic is applicable to us and to everything in the Universe. If HE (Narayana) brings the activity in us through various demigods, we perform the activities, else no activities at all. The entire Universe is a puppet in the hands of Narayana, who is the real puppeteer.

**Aatma has no wherewithal to perform any activity**

Vedanta says Aatma in the human body resides in the heart and the heart beats involuntarily on its own. He has no control over it, as the breathing is under the control of Mukhya Prana (MP) who is in the 3rd Kaksha. MP at the 3rd Kaksha along with other 11 Pranas (Pancha Pranas and Pancha upa-Pranas being controlled by Aham

Prana) all residing in the 18th Kaksha, keep the body functioning, as it should. The sensory organs (nose, eyes, tongue, skin, and ears) influence the Manas. The demigods of the sensory organs will, in fact, seed the thoughts in the mind. They (demigods) will decide what kind of thought should come to the Manas based on the past Karmas. If the thought of eating an apple pie is the strongest among lots of thoughts, which arise in the mind, the legs, which are under the control of Jayanta and Samba, who are in the 16th Kaksha, will lead the body to the kitchen. Now, with the involvement of other demigods – Indra (Kaksha 8) & Daksha (Kaksha 10) for hands and other demigods, which control the mind, the apple pie is cooked.

If someone makes apple pie, what is his Aatma's involvement in it? Nothing. Similarly, when the apple pie is cooked, Indra makes the handpick the pie, puts it in the mouth and Varuna who is in 13th Kaksha helps chew the pie inside the mouth, salivate through the tongue and enjoy the taste of the apple pie. Apana Vayu – one of the Pancha Vayus, brings down the chewed apple pie into the stomach. The stomach is located below the heart (in which the Aatma resides) and has no direct link to it. Then where is Aatma's involvement in eating the apple pie? – Nowhere.

### How Aatma feels that he does everything?

Aatma only experiences the emotions got out of the bodily movement to the kitchen, cooking the apple pie and eating it, that's all. That emotional experience makes Aatma feel that he has done everything inside the body. It is this that brings in the miseries, as the fruits of Karma done by others will get attached to him. The reality is, Aatma does nothing. Rather, the Brahman does everything through the demigods.

### How work really happens?

For someone to work, the divine has to enable the environment that gives a person an opportunity to work. If a man is unable to find work despite trying, we now know to whom to point the finger at. It is the divine that is not fetching him the job, however, when his time comes, the same divine will get that person a job that he deserves.

Giving him the job to do is not enough; the divine has to make him work by literally working on the job by itself. So, the credit or blame for the work should go to the divine itself and not to the person who is perceived to have done the job. Now, this should bring more clarity to the doership.

### What happens if we identify ourselves as the real doers?

Identifying ourselves as the doers of Karma brings lots of troubles to us. First of all, it comes out of ignorance – lack of true knowledge about doership. To complete our work, we would have knowingly or unknowingly brought mental or physical pain to many people or cause inconvenience to them and that brings issues to us. Let's know a bit more about this.

For example, let's consider a company is laying off employees as an order from the CEO due to the lower revenues and profits. The board of directors and CEO collectively take the decision; the CEO passes the orders to the HR Manager who in turn passes the order to lay off the employees to the HR executives. The HR executives will make sure this happens on the ground.

The laid-off employees may develop deep frustration. Some may even have anxieties of not finding the jobs for months as not finding jobs means unable to bring food to their dinner table. The very thought of receiving house eviction orders from the courts can cause anxiety and distress. The anxiety leads to depression that may turn suicidal if not treated by the counsellors.

However, the onus of causing all the disorders to the laid-off employees and their families will go directly to anyone who feels he/ she did the job. The distressed employees are facing the problems because of their past life deeds. The divine may be punishing them by getting them laid off for the past misdeeds. But the trouble starts if anyone thinks he is the doer of the job.

By thinking that way, he takes the ownership for causing mayhem to the sacked employees. That is enough for the noose of the

Karma to fall on his neck and the wrath for the employees' plight will fall upon him and as a result, the Karmic forces will begin to haunt him. Its effect can be seen either in the same life or in the next.

So, by identifying ourselves as the doers of the Karmas, we will have to take the ownership or responsibility for bringing pain to the people. It is like the knife taking responsibility for a murder and pair of scissors taking responsibility for a surgery. In both the cases, the blame or the credit should go to those who used these instruments to kill or operate. Making the instruments accountable makes no sense at all. Similarly, the divine uses demigods to bring the activities in the humans. So, the fruits of these activities – Good OR Bad should go to the demigods, which in turn are used as instruments by the Brahman. Finally, the Brahman is the doer of everything, so bouquet OR brickbat should go to HIM only.

To burn those Karmic impressions, we will have to take birth, again and again, experiencing the pain and agonies repeatedly, which we could have simply avoided by not taking the ownership of doing the Karmas in the first place.

## What should be our attitude when we perform any action?

When we work by keeping the concept of "object and its image" in the back of our mind, we will be reminded of non-doership constantly. We should also remember from the earlier discussion that if we get to lay hands on any work, which means the divine brought the work to us. So it's GOD's work and we have to do it with utmost sincerity. This helps us execute our daily works detachedly, without any expectations. In a nutshell, we have to do every work as a duty of GOD with an obligation to finish it professionally. Whatever we deserve as the fruits of work, we should have the humility to accept it as his grace. Even if the outcome is negative, we should take it positively and continue doing work enthusiastically as ever. This should be our attitude. Let's understand this in a bit more detail through an example.

**Example**: -

Let's consider someone working on an IT software project in an IT company as a junior cadre software engineer. If he had to work with the concept of "Object & its mirror image" in mind, he will just work with the laser focus to complete his work professionally without expecting any returns. He will not even care for the appreciation from his superiors and he won't get excited if he gets any. So for the salary, he takes from the company, he is duty bound to deliver his services efficiently as an expert without any expectation. He knows that whatever he deserves from his work, the divine gives it at the right time. He is only focused on completing his work on time and will have the magnanimity to help his team members if they need it. He will also keep himself updated on the latest technologies on his own without waiting for anyone's help, with this, he is ahead of others when it comes to being up-to-date. Being with the time and technology is a must to stay relevant in the fast-changing world.

Despite all his hard work, sometimes it may appear that the management does not recognize, but the reality is, it is being noted, discussed and appreciated silently among themselves. So when the right time comes, the boy will get all the rewards he deserves. However, he will take these adulations and rewards not to the head, but to the heart and remains as modest as ever. He will feel it is GOD's grace and will stay grateful to the divine as ever. This is called Nishkaama Karma (NK).

To perform any action in the way of NK, one should clearly understand this eternal truth – "One always gets what he deserves not what he desires". While working, one is being constantly bugged by the following thoughts "Will I get recognition for my work OR someone will take away the credit for my work?" "What if someone takes the credit meant for me, would I stay relevant in the Organisation?" "How to safeguard it?"

However as per the truth, one need not panic that someone would take away what rightfully belongs to him. If he deserved it, he will get it for sure no matter how much others try to snatch it.

The statement "Early bird gets the worm" is not true. This is because even the early bird will only get to eat what is destined for her. She won't get to eat the worms meant for other birds since the divine has reserved food for each of them. If any bird comes late, the worm that is destined to be eaten by that bird will remain untouched by other birds. In case if the bird that arrived late didn't get any worm, that means, she didn't deserve worms at that point in time, that's all. On the contrary, if the early bird doesn't deserve any worm, she won't get to eat any despite being there early.

So, in a nutshell, if one gets what he desired, it is clear that what he desired coincided with what he deserved and when he deserved. If he didn't deserve, he would never get it no matter how much he tries.

Let's throw some light on this subject to understand a little bit more.

## **We get what we deserve not what we desire**

Man is obsessed with and bitten by "I", "Me", "Mine" syndrome, which is bringing all sorts of problems to him. There may be exceptions but most of the populace suffers from this syndrome. One's day-to-day activities are centered around these. The anxieties, restlessness, anger, rage, depressions, various diseases, etc. are the byproduct of these. Upanishads say, "Our birth happens for us to enjoy/ suffer from the past Karmas and add on new Karmas for the future births". Upanishads also guarantees what is destined – good OR bad, one is sure to get no matter what one does to stop it. They (Upanishads) explain this with an example – "Every grain of rice bears the name of the eater", it is that certain as to whose mouth each of the grain should go into OR whose stomach the grain is destined to reach and get digested.

So, what is destined to us – good OR bad, no one can ever steal or take it from us and it is that certain. The point is, what is to be got and when is predestined too, it can never ever change. So, we won't get what is not destined for us, no matter how much we try. At the same time, whatever is destined we won't get until the destined time hasn't come. We all have experienced this in our lives, still, we are not prepared to accept it and instead get back to the above-said syndrome of "I", "Me", "Mine" and suffer, that is strange.

Let us take an example to get clarity on what has been said above

Example 1

Let's consider someone, very passionate about starting a software business is finding it very difficult to raise funds, despite owning a patent for the concept. The reality is, if he deserves funding from an external agency to start his business, the money will come looking for him at the appropriate time. He doesn't have to go looking for the money though. That means, he will get introduced to a person who has money and is looking for the right business idea to invest. When the right time comes, the matching happens and the money flows into the business. This happens even if there are thousands of business ideas from others to choose from since the match is made in heaven and both deserve each other.

On the contrary, if that person who has a patented idea doesn't deserve funding for his business, no matter how "earth-shattering" the business idea could be, not a single penny will come to him. That's the reality, one has to understand this truth and live.

Since the future is always a mystery to everyone, he still has to detachedly make serious attempts to source the funds while not being fixated on this task permanently.

He should do the work with the attitude "If it happens, good else no hard feelings. Maybe I don't deserve it. GOD has some other plans for me" and takes the outcome sportingly. This sticks to the truth "What is not destined one will never get it, no matter what. At the same time, what is destined, one will get no matter whatever is done to stop it". One should know this truth and live life accordingly.

Example 2

Likewise, let's consider a case where a person's desire to study and become a physician never materialized despite having all the credentials of becoming one. Many times, we may have everything but for GOD's grace, that's enough to scuttle the dream.

Sometimes the dream may turn into reality at the later stage of life OR it may never materialize due to the effects of past life Karmic impressions. In such cases, the deep desire to be a physician is etched permanently in the subconscious memory and stays there. However, it will surely materialize in one of the upcoming human births. If the divine will is not there, nothing happens. That is the reality.

**How is this kind of thinking linked to Nishkaama Karma (NK)?**

One of the reasons why we end up skipping to perform actions as the NK way is because of the anxiety that someone may covertly OR overtly steal what should rightly belong to us. The truth, however, is totally different; others can never snatch from us what is destined for us. Even if they appear to do so initially, eventually it will come back to us. So, if we do our duties with this awareness, it should put our fear and anxieties to permanent rest, while bringing inner peace. Once we are peaceful from the inside, we will be at peace with others from outside and this is a must to get the feeling of NK.

**How to practically apply this concept at work?**

We work in the offices and at times the credit of our hard work will go to someone who has not contributed much towards the work. Because of some political reasons, we may be compelled to accept it and continue the work despite knowing the fact that the other person will walk away with the credit.

But we, having earned the knowledge of NK, should develop the mindset to work enthusiastically as a service towards GOD. It is important to be in HIS good books and that should be our aim in life. Instead of going behind the returns of our work, we should get solidly behind the "responsibilities" of the job we are undertaking and try to meet OR exceed them.

The truth is, our good work, will never go unnoticed. It will certainly register in the minds and the good books of our superiors in the office. Though we don't get recognition immediately, we get it when our good time rolls in. Maybe, we will get more than what we had expected earlier. Recognitions come at the predestined time and not when we want it. What we must have is patience that's it. The divine knows what we deserve and when we should get it.

We have to keep this in our minds at the time of work to remain spirited even if someone else benefits from it. Also, constant remembrance about the "real object and its mirror image" can bring this spirit in us naturally.

When we perform all our actions like this, we will lose our animal instincts and our consciousness will elevate towards the divine. We will internally transform into yogis – Sthitha Prajna. Once we achieve this stage, from here our journey towards Moksha gets easy. One has to understand that achieving the state of Sthitha

Prajna is the hardest of all; too many hurdles to cross and only with the divine grace one can get it at a predestined time.

We must understand that everything in the Universe is predestined.

# Everything is predestined

**Is everything predestined?**

Some say everything is predestined and many allege it is not so, but partially preordained. Few claim nothing is fated, but we create everything out of our own thought process. So, which one is true? − To answer this, one has to just look at the society. In the society we see some are rich, some are poor, some are healthy some are diseased. Some are happy and some are sad. Some are lucky and some are unlucky and the list goes on and on. Why is there discrimination? If everything is our own making, why can't everyone create a life of his own and lead a rich and happy life? What is stopping them?

At the outset, everything appears as though we have choices in life and whatever happens in our lives is due to the wrong choices we make. But the question is, what makes us choose the wrong over right? − It's our fate.

The wisdom that is required to distinguish the right over wrong and the good over bad, fails at times and because of that, we end up taking wrong decisions in life. Now, who makes our wisdom fail? What causes its failure? − It's our fate again. During our good times, we tend to take the right decisions in life and all our efforts bear good results. For example, if we are in business and we are successful, the decision to start our own business itself is considered to be right and we tend to attract clients easily. That's when we say we are lucky and blessed.

Whereas, during our bad times, retaining customers will be a very big deal, let alone attracting new ones. So, what has changed? – Nothing, other than our fate. Our judgment about some steps we took with respect to our business turns out to be faulty. Maybe, the new investments or the expansion of the existing business, so on and so forth, has brought us the failure in life.

So in a way, our own fate drove us to make bad decisions in life and fail. What drives our fate? - Our past Karmas. That means, the Ordainer tightly controls us and makes us pay for whatever bad we did in the past and at the same time, get rewarded for whatever good we did in the past.

## The universe is in the tight grip of divine

Vedanta speaks in volumes about how the Universe is very tightly controlled by Brahman. When the entire Universe is under HIS iron grip, how can any inhabitant OR any object which is a part of the Universe, not be under the same iron grip? - ask the Vedas.

Although the Universe looks chaotic, there is orderliness behind it. Every event in the Universe is timed and works with clock precision. So that nothing can ever go wrong.

## Infinitely complex mathematics is behind the creation

Infinitely complex Vedic mathematics is behind the creation of time duration. From the smallest time in microseconds – to the largest time in trillions of years have been defined.

| Unit | Definition | Duration |
|---|---|---|
| *Paramāṇu* | Base unit | ≈ 26.3 μs |
| *Aṇu* | 2 Paramāṇu | ≈ 52.67 μs |
| *Trasareṇu* | 3 Aṇu | ≈ 158 μs |
| *Truṭi* | 3 Trasareṇu | ≈ 474 μs |
| *Vedha* | 100 Truṭi | ≈ 47.4 ms |
| *Lava* | 3 Vedha | ≈ 0.14 s |
| *Nimeṣa* | 3 Lava | ≈ 0.43 s |
| *Kṣaṇa* | 3 Nimesha | ≈ 1.28 s |
| *Kāṣṭhā* | 5 Kṣaṇa | ≈ 6.4 s |
| *Laghu* | 15 Kāṣṭhā | ≈ 1.6 min |
| *Danda* | 15 Laghu | ≈ 24 min |
| *Muhūrta* | 2 Danda | ≈ 48 min |
| *Ahorātram* (Day) | 30 Muhūrta | ≈ 24 h |
| Masa (Month) | 30 Ahorātram | ≈ 30 days |
| Ritu (Season) | 2 Masa | ≈ 2 months |
| Samvatsara (Year) | 2 Ayana | ≈ 365 days[4] |
| Ahorātram of Deva | | |

Note: μs = 1 micro second, ms = millisecond

S = second, Min = 1 minute.

**Yugas**: Yuga in Hinduism is an epoch or era within a four-age cycle. A complete Yuga starts with the Krita Yuga via Treta Yuga and Dwapara Yuga into Kali Yuga. Our present era is Kali Yuga, which started in 3102 BCE, with the end of the Mahabharata war at a place called Kurukshetra. Let's get a sneak peek into each of the Yugas

- Krita Yuga – This Yuga is for the period of 1,728,000 solar years.
- Treta Yuga – This Yuga is for the period of 1,296,000 solar years.
- Dwapara Yuga – This Yuga is for the period of 864,000 solar years.
- Kali Yuga – This Yuga is for the period of 432,000 solar years.

MahaYuga is the summation of all the 4 Yugas, which is equal to 43,20,000 solar years.

## Yuga calculations

- Dwapara Yuga is 2 times Kali Yuga, 2 x 432,000 = 864,000 solar years
- Treta Yuga is 3 times Kali Yuga, 3 x 432,000 = 1,296,000 solar years
- Krita Yuga is 4 times Kali Yuga, 4 x 432,000 = 1,728,000 solar years.

MahaYuga – The four Yugas constitute one MahaYuga and equal 4.32 billion solar years.

**Manvantara**: - 71 ChaturYugas constitute one Manvantara (30,67,20,000 solar years) and 14 Manvantaras put together to form 1 Chaturmukha Brahma Kalpa (4.32 billion solar years). Every Manvantara has one Manu as the predecessor of the human race who will live in that Manvantara – duration (time taken for the wheel of ChaturYuga to turn 71 times). Manu – a demigod, rules each Manvantara and the present Manu is "Vaivaswata Manu", who was the first man to walk on the earth in this Manvantara and hence the present Manvantara called "Vaivaswata Manvantara", which is the 28th one and another 43 remaining for the CBK.

**Chaturmukha Brahma Kalpa (CBK):** - 1000 MahaYuga makes one CBK, which is equal to 4.32 billion solar years and by then Chaturmukha Brahma's (CB) one day (12 hours) passed. There are a few dissolutions and the earth will get completely annihilated. It will remain in this state for another 4.32 billion years, which is the night of the CB but the Universe still remains intact.

**Brahma Ratra** (BR) – 2 x CBK is called BR, which is equal to 8.64 billion years, which is 24 hours of CB.

**Brahma Varsha** (BV) – BR x30x12 gives one year of CB, which is 8.64 billion years x 30 x 12.

**Brahma Para Ardha** (BPA) – BVx50, which is the 50 years of CB. As of now, the age of CB is past 50 years already and CB's one second is 100,000 solar years.

**Brahma Para Kaala** (BPK) – when BV is multiplied 100 times, it takes 100 years of CB, which is BV x 100. The complete age of the Universe is one BPK, which is 351,040,000,000,0000 solar years. The Universe once created will see activities for these many long years, which is also the lifespan of CB. He is the first Aatma to come into the material Universe through the mortal body to do Saadhana and hence is the last Aatma to lose it to attain Moksha after the Saadhana is completed. So, CB once taken birth at the time of Universal creation, will live this long and die to attain Moksha. In contrast, other Aatmas will come and go through the cycle of birth and death many times. However, the number of times they come and go depends on the kaksha at which they are located. After completing the BPK period, the Universe gets totally destroyed that it reaches the ionic state at the end of destruction.

Then it stays that way for another one BPK, that is another 351,040,000,000,0000 solar years without any activity and after that creation starts again.

Vedanta says it is night time (12 hours) of Narayana. The next creation is for another 1 BPK; it is daytime (12 hours) for the Brahman OR Narayana. The philosophers state this symbolically, to explain the infiniteness of the Narayana. In reality, HE is beyond birth and death and hence is beyond time. HE is ever existing, never changing infinite consciousness OR energy.

When everything and every event in the Universe are timed, planned and executed under tight control to make it work exactly as envisaged, where is the room for freedom? When start and end events are already pre-decided for the Universe, then the events in between them should also be pre-decided, else it is not a science at all.

## Solar system – complex machinery at work

The control of the Universe is not complete if our solar system is not in the direct control of Brahman OR divine. Each of the 9 planets with their satellites revolves around the sun at a predetermined speed, which is controlled by the divine. The satellites also orbit their native planets at different speeds, again pre-decided by the divine. So, everything seems to be planned and executed at clock precision. That's exactly the reason why we have seasons, night and day happening, 365 days without giving a miss. Due to the phenomena like seasons, days & nights and solar & lunar energies, waxing, waning of the moon and many others, we have life on earth. Any minor distortion in the otherwise precisely working of the heavenly bodies will result in the catastrophe, which in turn results in the loss of life in massive proportions. So, the divine will never-ever let anything go out of control, no matter what. From the movements of electrons around the nuclei of the atoms to the orbiting of gigantic cosmic bodies in the cosmos, everything is planned and executed with clock precision, hence nothing can ever go wrong.

When the situation is like this, how can anyone say the man has the freedom to do his own things?

Let's delve more into it with local examples

The same is true with many things we experience in our lives on a day-to-day basis. The local trains, which ply in cities, will have departure and arrival times fixed. For example, let's consider a train traveling between stations A and E, A -> B ->C ->D ->E. The departure time is fixed at the station A and the arrival time at E is also fixed. When this is the case, the driver of the train will have no option other than driving at the speed mentioned in the manual. He has no freedom to drive at his will. For the train to arrive at a particular time at station E, the speed of the train, as well as duration of the stoppages at in-between stations, are also pre-decided and fixed. The driver has to just stick to the plan and has no freedom at all to deviate from it.

The train is not only depending on the driver but also on many things – The infrastructure – reliable electricity, quality railings and many more, to support the flawless movement of trains. So, those who work for maintaining the quality of the infrastructure also are bound by the rules and they too cannot deviate from standard procedures. If all these dependencies are handled well, then the train journey will be smooth and flawless. In this setup, anyone agency not sticking to the plan means, the train meeting up with accidents and subsequent loss of life. So, when a simple train journey has everything pre-planned and superbly executed as per the plan without any deviations, what about the Universe? – That too should have a plan; else the Universe won't function the way it should.

Example

We get our house built with our hard earned money. Before we start building, we get the plan OR the blueprint for the whole house ready. The blueprint will talk about the following:

- The overall area the house that occupies on the ground.
- Built up area
- Number of rooms the house will have
- The dimensions of each room

- Information about bathrooms, so on and so forth.

When we have all the information, that's when we can have the detailed plan ready for the house. After that, we would be able to estimate how much it would cost to build it.

Now imagine if we say, "We have a plan for everything except for the master bedroom, which we shall decide once the construction is in full swing", will it make any sense? We never know for sure, how big the master bedroom should be - the interiors of the room, the dimension of the attached bathroom and its interiors, etc. Without the prior knowledge of all these, how can we start the construction work? If we begin the construction work also, it will be held up due to lack of a full plan. To work on the full plan, we should have sub-plans ready too. The Sub-plans are the plans for each of the rooms, bathrooms, garden area, garbage disposal area, provision for bringing power and water into the house from the source. Like these, there are many more things we should give attention to before we take up building the house.

In a nutshell, we can't build a house, unless we have the full blueprint for the entire house. Also, when there is a plan, it is the owner of the house who will freeze it. The builders – engineers, work supervisors, labourers don't have rights to change the plan in the way they want. If they do, the house won't be of what the owner wanted, it would be something else. So, in order to build the house exactly as the owner envisaged, they (builders) will stick to the plan, that's it.

When a simple logic like this is applicable to the building of a house, what makes us think it is not applicable to the Universe?

At the time of creation of the Universe, the divine made a meticulously planned, detailed blueprint of the Universe. The Universe works based on that divine plan without any deviations and the main plan has infinite pre-decided sub-plans. Every sub-plan is carefully executed so that nothing ever goes awry even for a second.

The sub-plans are for all the inhabitants of the Universe – all cosmic bodies, living beings, plant kingdom, so on and so forth. We, as humans form one of the inhabitants of the Universe and have a sub-plan made for us by the divine. So the divine controls our life based on our past Karmas. It is so from the time we came into the Universe by falling into the cycle of birth and death until we permanently escape from it in the end. Moreover, everything in the Universe, including us, is the divine reflection. We are the reflected image of the divine, which is a true object. So, we will only do what the divine makes us do and our life is in absolute control of GOD.

Hence, every event in our life is decided and executed methodically as envisaged by the divine and we don't have any say in it. If any event happened as per our wish, it is to be concluded that the event was in the divine's sub-plan. Divine too wished that the event should happen that way. So, our will and the divine will coincide at last.

This being the case in life, all we have to do is, submit to the infinite power with humility, that's it. That's when we are able to cross any thunderstorm that hits our life with ease.

**Life is a puppetry**

Since our life is in the hands of GOD, he makes us do things as a puppeteer uses his strings to play puppetry. Let's look into it in a bit detail.

**Example**

We don't know from where we came? Why we came? Who chose the mother's womb? Where will we go when we die? – We have no answers though but one point to note is, as soon as we are born, the divine fixes everything for us, like which school and college we should go to, in what subject should we graduate from, which profession we should choose, if it is a job, then which company should we work for, if business, what kind of business have we to do, whom to marry, who should be born as our off-springs, so on and so forth.

The list is endless, it includes the following: should we live healthily OR should we be diseased. When, where, at what time and how should we meet our death? Being the real object, GOD makes everything happen to the mirror image, that is us. So, everything will happen, as it should, we don't have control over it.

## **Logical analysis of controlled human life**

Example 1: - Let's throw some more light on this topic through the following example. We shall consider someone whose life-long aspiration of becoming an internationally reputed pianist never materialized. He may have all the credentials to become a pianist, but for God's grace OR luck. Since he didn't have luck, he never got an opportunity to become one. It was due to his fate, which in turn is driven by the past Karmic impressions.

He dies with this unfulfilled desire etched in his subconscious mind. However, in his next life, his wish will be granted, as his negative Karmic impressions are burnt off in his present life.

In the next life, the person shows an affinity towards music right from the childhood days. The divine will make things smoother for him by creating the right environment for that. His grades and other factors, which decide his eligibility to the internationally reputed music school, will favour him. Even the funds for financing his education will get tied up easily without much effort. To say the least, when divine decides to turn him into a musician, it doesn't matter how poor the boy is, everything will fall into place for him. One day he will be a musician – internationally revered pianist and that's it.

Now let's see if he has any choice of not becoming a pianist. Let's assume, though he has an inclination for studying music, his parents force him to study and become an attorney. But as destiny wants it, all his doors of opportunity for becoming an attorney starts shutting one after another for him. His marks/ grades won't favour admission into any law college. So an environment will get created in such a way that either he has to take up music course OR quit studying altogether. He is cornered in such a way that he has no choice but to embrace music as his profession. This is how the divine will arm twist and make him do what it wants, at last.

Example 2

Let's say someone is destined to die at the age of 81 by being run over by a truck while crossing a road, as his death is pre-decided that way. The event depends on the time at which he hits the road and the time at which the truck comes to the same spot. Both the times should match perfectly and that's when the run-over happens. Now, if the person comes late or early even by a few seconds, the accident won't happen. This is true with the truck also, if the truck comes to the spot either late OR early by a few seconds, the truck will miss him.

So there should be someone who is meticulously coordinating this event and it is the Brahman in the form of "GOD of Death". HE will make sure the run-over happens and the person dies on the spot because the individual is destined to die that way.

Suppose if the freedom to the person and the truck driver is given, then there is 50% chance of his death. But if he misses his death, there is nothing further written in the story of his life. The man has no reason to live; his story is supposed to end with the death through the run-over.

It is exactly like a film. With the ending of the story, the movie also ends. Just because the audience liked the movie and want to have the storyline extended, they don't get to watch the movie furthermore. This is because a movie is based on a story. The story will have start and end to it and so it is with the movie.

Nothing lives, once the purpose for which it is created has been served, the divine itself will destroy it. In the case of living beings, the divine kills and that's it.

## **Everything is stage-managed**

Some say at every stage, life gives choices and depending on what we choose we create the rest. How to answer this? It is true that life gives options but what we choose is not in our control. The truth is, the divine will pull the strings and make us choose – Good OR Bad, based on our past Karmas. Let's look into it a bit in detail

## Example

If perverted friends or classmates of a teenager going to a college introduce him to drugs, what should he do? - He has 2 choices, either he outrightly rejects it as taking drugs will ultimately result in self-destruction and death OR he embraces it by glossing over the pitfalls of taking drugs and suffer seriously in the future.

It appears as though the kid has 2 choices in front of him. On close observation, we can see it is not that black and white for the kid to decide. If the kid has a happy family at home with loving parents and siblings, the kid won't find it appropriate to go towards drugs, he opts to stay away from it.

On the contrary, a kid falls prey to drugs if he is not happy at home. This could be because the parents are not on good terms with each other. They constantly fight OR the boy maybe depressed because his sibling accidentally passed away. He may be constantly ridiculed/ bullied at home by his siblings/ parents/ friends and due to that, he may be depressed. In such scenarios, he will not bother about the self-destruction due to the drug abuse and rather proceed to tread that path.

What makes us choose right over wrong OR good over bad? - It is our wisdom. However, our wisdom depends on the circumstances under which we have to make decisions, which in turn depends on the environment we are living in.

## Who creates the environment for everyone?

The divine creates it based on the past Karmas. Suppose if the kid has to suffer and finally die because of drugs due to his past misdeeds, the divine would create the second type of environment. If not, it would create the first type of environment.

How does the divine make us take wrong steps in life?

It does that by turning off the switch of wisdom, which is essentially required for us to do the reasoning before taking any step in life. Lack of wisdom means, committing mistakes - silly to serious ones in life and seriously suffer from the losses later. Similarly, when our good times come, the divine turns-on the switch of wisdom for us so that we take right/ timely decisions and reap the good harvest. The divine does either of the two based on our past Karmas.

## Divine creates the environment for controlling everything

We read in the earlier chapters that divine controls everything in the Universe by creating the necessary environment for it. Let's see how he does it.

For example, we all know that life is dependent on the monsoons, which is under the absolute control of the divine. The divine builds the environment as follows:

Using solar energy, water from all the water-bodies especially the oceans is evaporated during the summer months and the water-bearing clouds are formed offshore over the oceans. The summer sunshine heats up the landmass, creating the temperature difference between land and the oceans. The high temperature on the onshore and low temperature offshore will result in pressure differentials. That is low pressure onshore and high pressure offshore. This pressure difference is good enough for the water-bearing clouds to move towards onshore at very high speed driven by gusts of winds. The trees, hills and other structures Enroute will facilitate the water stored in the ionic form on the clouds, to precipitate and come down as rains. The clouds move from high-pressure, low-temperature area to low pressure, high-temperature areas. Whichever cities/ towns/ villages the divine intends to shower with rains, HE creates adequate temperature and pressure differences there, so heavy rains lashes over. Wherever HE wishes no rains, HE will never create the required environment there. So clouds bypass these areas altogether resulting in low rains OR no rains at all. This is how HE creates the environment and stage-manages the show.

Similarly, if divine wishes someone to rise in his career and become the head of an MNC, first it creates the enabling environment for that. Automatically the person starts attracting right kind of people to work with him. He will be the darling of the clients. His leadership abilities and potential to motivate people to get due recognition. His competency in problem-solving during any crisis will be the talk of the organization. Slowly he will rise in the organization by taking more and more responsibilities and achieving big, which is admired by the leadership team of the company.

So within a predestined time period, he will break the glass ceiling and will eventually get into the shoes of CEO of that organization.

For that to happen, the divine gave the person, the competent people to work with him, the right kind of wisdom, a sharp intellect, an effective communication power, the leadership capabilities, appreciation from the clients, respect from colleagues and the charisma of a CEO, to become one. With all these, finally, the person achieves what the divine wished.

Things work in the opposite direction if divine wishes someone in high place fall in life and bite the dust. This is how the divine sets the environment first and absolutely controls everything as per the plan in the Universe. This shows, how the seemingly independent lives of ours are truly controlled by the divine, without leaving any trace of it.

Vedanta says the purpose of human birth is to attempt to get liberated from the noose of the cycle of death and birth and attain moksha as fast as one can. This is because birth means a combination of pain and pleasure induced by the past Karmas and addition of some more Karma in the present life, thus triggering more births. So, it is a vicious circle that one has to break with force to move ahead and achieve Moksha at all cost.

### Does the "philosophy of predestination" encourage idleness?

The theology – "everything is predestined" can promote neither idleness nor laziness because one can laze around only if he knows his future. If not, his instinct will never let him laze. We have seen this in our lives, yet I want to explain it through examples.

Example1

Someone who wants to go to a city, which is a faraway place, can be at rest and laze only if he has already booked his seat in the bus and knows the departure time of the bus. Now let's imagine that he has to go to another far away city and he couldn't book his seat due to some strange reasons and he is not sure of the departure time of the bus. Though the truth "if he is destined to travel comfortably, he will get a seat in the bus" is still applicable, will his instinct ever keep him in peace OR laze around? – NO, never. He will get restless and will do everything to somehow get a seat on the bus by going early to the bus stop.

Life is also like that, though we know that one day we all have to die and go away leaving behind everything – name, fame, money, property, family, yet our instinct will still make us believe that we live forever and make us attached to everything we seem to possess. Because of the attachment, we behave as if we are going to live forever and keep doing things.

Example2

There is saying, "If someone is destined to get hit and run over by a speeding vehicle, it happens at all cost, else it never happens". This theology of predestining is true, with this in mind, how many of us are ready to cross any busy road with closed eyes? – No one. Our instincts won't allow us to do that. It is the same with everything in our lives. We can't sit and wait with the understanding that if we are destined to get something we will somehow get it, else we won't. Rather we try our best to get it on our own. Our instinct will push us to do that. So, this being the case, where is the question of idling around?

We shall know the purpose of human birth next.

## The purpose of life

The philosophers of the yore claimed that life is a preparation for death. Death is certain that everyone – the rich, the poor, the prince, the peasant, the accomplished, the unaccomplished and so on have to embrace one day. No one ever has taken anything at the time he departed by bidding "goodbye" to life and it remains so till date. It will remain the same into the eternity. In this context when we look at life, everything appears superficial. Our struggles, anxieties, anger, bloated egos, our insecurities, etc. have no meaning as everything is predetermined. We only get what we deserve, never what we desire. This being the eternal truth, we have to perform every action as a divine duty and wholeheartedly accept the outcome of our work as HIS grace. This is so because we have no other choice. So, overly-excited with the positive outcome and depressed-to-the-core upon the negative outcome of our work, won't help us in any way. It will bring us anxiety and pushes us deep into depression. So, maintaining equanimity in life is an absolute must as it is this quality of mind that will give us lasting mental peace and happiness.

One point we should understand is, everything in life is temporary in nature, be it good OR bad. It has to pass one day. In fact, life itself is a temporary phenomenon and we never know when we lose it. No one knows when he dies, as GOD has kept one's death in the deepest dark. Death is a top secret the divine maintains in order to avoid the death related fear and anxieties.

All these narrations are nice to hear, however, it is easier said than done to implement it in life. Also, truth always tastes bitter and is very difficult for one to digest. Nevertheless, it is nearly impossible to accept the negative outcomes of our work sportingly.

<u>So, how to go about it?</u> - When we clearly understand the purpose of life, we will be able to achieve this in our lives.

## Does life have any purpose?

Human life is not by accident; there is a reason why we are here and life has a meaning. Not only life has a purpose, even the creation has one too. In fact, nothing happens without any purpose in the Universe.

In our lives too, this rule is applicable and we don't notice it, that's all. For example, from the time we wake up from sleep until we sleep at night, we are constantly doing some work or the other. When we analyze, we can clearly see the purpose behind every work of ours. Let's dive deep into it to understand.

<u>Example</u>

We go to the office to work and the purpose behind it is to earn money for a living. We eat food and we want it tasty too but the purpose behind eating is enjoying the taste of food and filling our stomach. We watch TV soaps, movies and the purpose behind it is to entertain ourselves. We go for brisk walks, we do yoga, pranayama, and meditation; the true purpose behind these activities is to keep ourselves nimble and fit. We stand in line at an ATM counter; the purpose is to withdraw cash. We sleep at night and the purpose behind is to get rest and get ready for the next day's activities. We take bath to cleanse our bodies and keep them tidy. We wear expensive, stylish clothes and the purpose is to look and feel good in front of others. We buy a house and live in it to feel secure - physically and financially and the list is endless.

Like this, we do all our works with a clear purpose in mind but we don't ever question if life itself has any purpose – The scriptures say, "Life not only has a purpose but living has a meaning too." Also, they add, "The Purpose of life is GOD realization". So, it is wise to start concentrating on realizing GOD very early in life, to avoid additional Karmic impressions getting attached to us. Lesser the number of births, better it is as we get to live in communion with GOD that much earlier.

However, we are humans with the logical mind and sometimes we get a question in mind as to why we should bother about GOD realization? We are anyway doing fine with good health, prosperous life, and happy family. Why break our head over Karmas? We may rather feel that maintaining the status quo should make more sense than breaking our head over who is the real doer? Why should we bother about performing every action in the NK way? - The point is, the present life is just one out of the millions of lives we have gone through so far and the millions we will go through in the future, as a result of Karmic impressions. Since no one knows how painful life is going to be and what kind of agony we have to face in the coming births, it is better to do something to avoid OR reduce the sufferings in the future lives.

So, instead of getting intoxicated with the superficial pleasure that the present life is offering, we have to answer the question "What's next in life?" This is because, everything has to end one day, including life. Questioning consistently about life will eventually open our eyes to the temporariness of everything life has to offer.

Also, there are consequences for everything we do - good or bad. We should know that every birth triggers a minimum of 14 births - both human and non-human and this is despite leading a cautious life of detached attachment. Now, imagine, what will happen if we lead our lives fully attached, chasing the sensory gratification? - The result is attachments. In fact, more attached we get in life, more pain we suffer from, in the present as well as the future lives. More attachments lead to the accumulation of more Karmic impressions, which results in more births in the future.

So, instead of whiling away our precious time in the present life, we should lead lives in a way that creates lesser or no Karmic impressions. By leading a life of detached attachment and performing every action with the sense of NK, we will be able to achieve it. However, it won't happen in one life itself, but it will mark the beginning of our conscious journey towards GOD because the kingdom of GOD OR Vaikunta is the final resting place for all God-loving Aatmas.

Let's analyze Karmas briefly and find out what the Holy Scriptures have got to say.

## Karmas

There are 3 types of Karmas

- **Sanchita Karma**

    These Karmas are impressions of the past Karmas – the ones accumulated in the past lives, which are to be burnt off. This can be warded off lightly through the grace of the divine.

- **Prarabda Karma**

    These are Karmic impressions of past lives, which are being experienced by the Aatma currently. This has to be burnt off without any alternatives. If the Aatma has submitted internally and externally to the divine with humility, then the divine out of pity may give the wherewithal to experience the pain, that's it.

- **Aagami Karma**

    These are the Karmic impressions, which will come into force in the coming lives. These impressions are the result of Karmas performed in the present life. Those Karmas performed mentally also add to the list. Experiencing the Karmic backlashes of these Karmas can be completely prevented when the Aatma submits to the divine with absolute humility.

With this information in mind when one looks at life, that's when he realizes the dangers of leading a life of sensory gratification. Also, performing actions through deep attachments is like playing with fire; there is a likelihood of one getting seriously burnt accidentally. So, one should lead a life of detached attachment and be duty bound throughout, to make sure Karmas are performed but impressions are not created in life.

## Is divine grace required to bring a sense of DA in life?

It is humanly not possible for one to constantly be aware of non-doership and perform every action detachedly in the form of NK. To do that, one needs exclusive skills, which Krishna says in the Bhagavad Geetha, that it can only come from HIS (Krishna's) exclusive grace to the individual. So, it boils down to the divine's grace for someone to bring this feeling in life, which will eventually result in the person performing activities through the way of NK.

How to invoke divine grace? – The scriptures claim that one can invoke the divine grace through divine love. However, the love for the divine cannot come just like that. It can only come when one has the right knowledge of the divine. That means a person should understand the infinitely powerful, infinitely knowledgeable, all-pervading yet infinitely merciful divine to his capacity. Why only to his capacity? – This is so because one cannot understand GOD in entirety. Our finite human intellect can never grasp the infinite GOD, no matter how much we try. GOD has infinite attributes and each attribute is infinitely deep (bottomless). So, let alone understanding the infinite qualities of the divine, even understanding of one single attribute fully is not possible. This is true with even demigods, who lack the wherewithal to understand the divine fully. Saint Madhvacharya records in his works that only Lord Narayana knows about HIMSELF fully, because only an infinite mind can fully understand an infinite being. So even Lakshmi, HIS eternal consort, has a limited understanding of HIM. Vedas claim Brahman is the essence of everything, as HE makes all things happen. The flowers bloom because of HIM. The fruits ripen because of HIM and they taste exactly how they should, due to HIS grace. This one attribute of blooming of flowers and ripening of fruits in itself is so infinitely complex, that limited human intelligence can never grasp it fully. Like this, there is a very infinitely long list of activities (from micro to macro levels) happening 24x7 on the planet earth and the divine is behind each one of them.

If the earth itself is this complex then imagine the activities happening on the other 8 planets of our solar system. What about ones happening inside our SUN? What about all the activities happening in our milky way? This is getting ridiculously endless and no amount of our intelligence can ever crack all of these.

So, how to go about it now? – Again only through HIS grace, one will understand the divine to one's capacity. How to invoke HIS grace? - The deep desire and the humility required to understand GOD is an absolute must for the grace. We have seen that, what we desire deeply, we will attract it. This includes the divine grace, which in turn results in the divine knowledge. The divine love and knowledge will bring the sense of detachment in us, as all other things start appearing to us "superficial" when compared to the ecstasy of the divine bliss.

However, one will get the divine knowledge through several lives as the person also has to simultaneously burn the past impressions in each life. So, the time available in each life is very limited, so it prolongs GOD-realisation.

However, the more a man understands the divine, the more he will fall in love with it and more he wants to know about it. This gets into the addiction to the divine, which pushes him deep into detachment. The detachment is the prerequisite of NK.

When a man performs every action detachedly through NK, he is said to be doing it, as a service to the Lord and that's when his regular work becomes worship for him.

This way, his consciousness rises to the divine level and one day he will have GOD-realization. After that, he is liberated from the distress and the pain caused by the cycle of birth-and-death. Once he is out of the cycle of birth-and-death, he is free to attain moksha, again only with the divine grace.

## Do all Aatmas attain Moksha?

To answer this question, we should understand the nature of Aatma

- **Nature of Aatma**

    We have seen in the earlier chapters that Aatmas have GUNAs OR nature. That means, every Aatma has its own nature, which makes it unique from the others.

    An Aatma can be compared loosely to the seed of a fruit, which also has its own unique nature that gives the distinct taste, aroma, colour, nutrition, size and shape for that fruit. The nature of the fruit is so unique, that no two fruits even from the same tree are 100% alike in all the aspects described above. There is a difference and it's just that the human tongue is not equipped to differentiate the small variation in taste between the fruits. Similarly, the eyes are not powerful enough to make out the very minute differences in shape, size, and colour between the fruits. So, in a nutshell, every fruit is unique from the other and so is everything in the creation.

- **The Guna of an Aatma**

    However, Aatmas have consciousness but the seeds don't. The Aatmas are further classified as Satvik, Rajasik, and Tamasik. Sathvik Aatmas are the lovers of divine and help to maintain the universal order, whereas Tamasik Aatmas hate the divine and try to oppose OR break the universal law and order. Rajasik Aatmas are neither divine lovers nor divine haters. They love themselves and are extremely greedy and self-centered

- **The final destination of Aatmas**

    Every Aatma is on an eternal perpetual journey. Some move towards the Infinity, in the direction of light, some move away from the infinity, towards darkness. That means the evolution of human consciousness is continuous and across lives. It is compared to the seemingly unending journey towards the infinite GOD for those Aatmas seeking the light. The journey is in the opposite direction for those seeking darkness.

    The evolution of light seeking Aatmas, however, is from animal to human to divine instincts. But for darkness seeking Tamasik Aatmas, the evolution is in the opposite direction.

The saint Madhvacharya in his works says, of all Aatmas under Kshara Purusha category, only the Satvik ones, at the end of their evolution, will reach Narayana – the source of all lights. The Tamasik Aatmas, on the contrary, will move away from HIM, into Andam Tamas – the source of all kinds of darkness.

However, Rajasik Aatmas will neither move towards light nor towards darkness because they never get liberated from the cycle of birth-and-death in the first place. This is because their evolution is not linear but circulatory and hence never in one direction. They keep coming back to earth, do Karmas and experience the fruits of them – good and bad. Upon burning the karmic impressions, they come back to do more Karmas. This goes on into eternity.

- **Moksha OR Vaikunta for Sathvik Aatmas**

    The saint Madhvacharya in his works describes that only Sathvik Aatmas will attain Moksha once their Saadhana is over. Saadhana, for an Aatma, is the disciplined and dedicated practice (physical & mental) to become a perfect human and to acquire spiritual knowledge to his/ her full capacity.

    Since each Aatma is unique, which is reflected in the individual's personality by his nature. Also, his mental capacity is unique too. We say the sea is full; the well is full; the tank is full; the pot is full; the river is full yet the fullness of each is different, asserted Madhvacharya. Likewise, Aatmas have their individual fullness too. Those at the top Kakshas have more capacity to fill when compared to those at the lower Kakshas.

- **The capacity of an Aatma**

    Chaturmukha Brahma and Mukhya Prana at Kaksha 3 have more capacity and potential when compared to Saraswati and Bharathi who are at the Kaksha 4. Hence, their Saadhana is more compared with those of Saraswati and Bharathi.

    Garuda, Sesha and Rudra who are at Kaksha 5, have more capacity and potential when compared to their respective eternal consorts Sauparni, Vaaruni and Paarvati who are at Kaksha 7. Hence, their Saadhana is more, compared with those of Sauparni, Vaaruni, and Paarvati.

**Aatmas and their Saadhana**

The Saadhana for the Aatmas at the higher Kakshas is much higher, intense than those at the lower Kakshas.

- **Bliss of Aatmas**

    Bliss at Moksha is different for each Aatma, which is based on his degree of knowledge and spiritual perfection. It is also linked to his inherent capacity and the Kaksha he belongs to.

    Chaturmukha Brahma and Mukhya Prana at Kaksha 3 experience more bliss when compared to Saraswati and Bharathi who are at the Kaksha 4. The difference in the bliss goes on with respect to Kakshas at which each OR the group of Aatmas reside.

Nevertheless, the divine through the grace grants Moksha OR Vaikunta to the Aatmas.

- **<u>Andam Tamas for Tamasik Aatmas</u>**

    Saint Madhvacharya states in his works that Tamasik Aatmas will never reach Vaikunta – the kingdom of Lord Narayana. Instead, they reach an eternal (subtlest) hell called Andam Tamas, in which they reside for eternity. They experience pain based on the Kaksha they reside. They won't reach the divine because their nature is evil. Thinking badly and harming the others, taking revenge, feeling jealous, greediness, lusting others' women/ men, stealing, being corrupt and the list of evilness goes on and on. In fact, the negativity is inherent in their nature, which can never be erased at all.

This is similar to the bitterness of the bitter gourd. Being bitter is in the nature OR quality of that vegetable. It cannot be changed, no matter how much sugarcane juice is poured into the plant while harvesting.

- **Pain at Andam Tamas**

    The pain experienced by Tamasik Aatmas at Andam Tamas depends on the Kaksha at which each Aatma is located.

    The pain experienced by each of the Tamasik Aatmas depends on how evil they are. The super-evil Kalee who is at highest Kaksha, experiences the maximum pain. Alakshmi, his eternal consort, who is 100 times less evil than him, experiences 100 times less painful than him. Similarly, Viprachitti is 100 times less evil than Alakshmi, hence experiences 100 times less pain and it goes on like this.

- **The final destination of Rajasik Aatmas**

    The Rajasik Aatmas are neither divine lovers nor divine haters. They just love themselves the most and hence they are self-centric. It is because of their Guna, their final destination is the material Universe itself. They will never escape from the jaws of birth and death and stay stuck with it forever.

## Number of births is pre-destined

The layers of impurities – Karmic impressions, attached to the Aatmas vary from one another. So is the number of births required to burn it.

The Brahman controls everything, including the eternal journey of Aatmas towards the Moksha/ light OR towards Andam Tamas/ darkness. That means the number of births the Sathvik Aatmas have to take for attaining Moksha is pre-decided. Similarly, the number of births that Tamasik Aatmas have to take to attain Andam Tamas is also pre-decided. However, it is not applicable for Rajasik Aatmas. They will never get out of birth-death cycle as they keep coming back every time the Universe is created. This is because they neither have divine qualities to attain Moksha NOR have asuric qualities to attain Andam Tamas. They are in between, so their eternal journey is not linear, rather circular.

## Pain OR pleasure we enjoy in life is to erase Karmic impressions

Like gold-ore needs complicated treatment to cleanse the ore impurities for extracting gold traces, Aatmas too need treatment to remove the impurities – traces of Karmas, for making them (Aatmas) glitter naturally. For example, if one ton of gold-ore has traces of 1 gram of gold, then to extract the same, the gold-ore is subjected to a particular type of complicated treatment. So, instead of 1 ton, if the ore size is 1.5 tons and the gold trace is more or less than 1 gram, the gold-ore is subjected to another type of complicated treatment. In both the cases the treatment given is different, complicated and elaborative so that at the end, every trace of impurities is removed.

Similarly, the treatment for Aatmas too varies. Since the number of impurities – traces of Karma, stuck around Aatmas varies, the kind of treatment an Aatma gets, also varies. GOD grants enough number of births for Aatmas to rid themselves off Karmic traces. In fact, the pain and pleasure the man experiences in life is a part of the treatment. Hence, one should accept it as the grace of GOD without fretting because the pain is the sign of Karmic purification. So, to put it in simple terms, the number of births for an Aatma is dependent on the layers of Karmic impurities attached to him OR her and it is predestined.

## The divine tightly controls the evolution of an Aatma through various births

Saint Madhvacharya has stated in his works that Aatmas always depend on Lord Narayana for their very existence as beings. It is so from the time immemorial to the eternity, even after they fully complete their evolution, that is, even in Moksha and Andam Tamas. However, when the Aatmas take birth in the material

Universe for the sake of doing Saadhana, HE controls them through the following means:

- Shrusti (creation OR birth)
- Sthithi (protection throughout life)
- Laya (destruction OR death)
- Jnana (knowledge OR wisdom)
- Ajnana (lack of knowledge OR wisdom)
- Bandha (entanglements)
- Muktha (release from entanglements)
- Moksha (liberation)

- **Shrusti**

    It means granting birth to an Aatma through a woman's womb. The divine will decide whose child and into which family an Aatma should be born.

- **Sthithi**

    It means governing the newborn child throughout life. It is the divine which decides what kind of education the child should get, what profession he should get into in his adulthood, whom he should marry and who all should be born as his children through his wife's womb, so on and so forth. That means everything is pre-decided.

- **Laya**

It means death. The divine decides how many years the individual should live and when his life should end and how it should end. At the end of his life, the divine destroys the person by killing him.

- **Jnana**

    It means wisdom OR knowledge (material and spiritual). The divine bestows upon wisdom and knowledge (material and spiritual) to the individual. Also, how much Jnana is appropriate to the individual in his present life is pre-decided by HIM, based on the past Karmas. If someone has the right wisdom, it is only due to HIS grace that's all.

- **Ajnana**

    It means lack of wisdom OR knowledge (material and spiritual). An individual is kept in Ajnana or darkness by the divine, based on the past Karmas. As a result, the person commits all kinds of blunders throughout his life and bears the brunt of it.

- **Bandha**

    It means entanglement. The divine puts an individual into entanglements in life by making him over-attached to everything he comes in contact and lives with. Though entanglements give pleasure to the individual at times, mostly they suffocate him later. The consequence of it is pain, which in turn is the result of the past Karmas.

- **Muktha**

    It means disentanglement. The divine releases the individual from all the entanglements by granting him the wisdom to stay detached in life. Detachment gives joy whereas attachment gives pain. Again the disentanglement happens as a result of past Karmas.

- **Moksha**

    It means permanently living in the kingdom of GOD – Vaikunta. When the Saadhana of an individual is complete - when all the Karmic impressions are burnt off and the Aatma has accumulated the spiritual knowledge to his full capacity, the divine bestows Moksha upon him.

## Should we stop doing our regular work and instead pursue GOD?

The Holy scriptures proclaim life's only purpose is to realize GOD. It is only through GOD Realisation that one can burn-off all his Karmic impressions, thus breaking his every link to the material Universe so that he can escape from the cycle of birth and deaths. So, one should pursue GOD to reach the kingdom of Lord at the earliest.

However, at times like now when we lead a busy life, where is the time for pursuing GOD? - Lord Krishna has an answer for this. Let's see what he has got to say.

Before the incarnation of Lord Krishna, in the bygone era over 5000 years ago, there was a belief that regular day-to-day works and those works, which are done to invoke divine grace, are different. The divine works involved performing a lot of complicated rituals, chanting mantras and so on. Those days when the conditions were totally different than what it is today, they could afford to lead their lives that way. However, the world changed much from that period over the years.

By the time Lord Krishna (LK) arrived, the world started becoming materialistic and dharma too had lost its sheen.

That's when LK's advice through the Bhagavad Geeta to treat every work as GOD's work made much sense to humanity. LK advice to Arjuna in BG, "What you do is not important to me, rather how you do, is". LK confided Arjuna to treat every work as a service to the lord and do it with a sense of duty, without any expectations. So through Arjuna, LK passed the message to mankind that always one should do his Karma as NK to invoke the divine blessings.

For any person, this advice came as blessing-in-disguise, as taking time off from his busy schedule to perform rituals for invoking GOD's grace was becoming increasingly difficult. Performing activities detachedly as a service to the divine itself is enough to win LK's heart.

This being the case, people can continue to do whatever they do as their profession. They should do it with the motto "Work is worship", that is enough. Even works outside of one's profession also need to be performed with the same mindset. When we make GOD, the most loved one and an integral part of our life, and then it becomes that much easier to do every work as a service to HIM.

Nevertheless, one has to exercise caution while selecting one's work. Any work, which is done to harm (emotionally OR physically) others, work done out of greediness and other activities which are done out of evil intentions, will never attract the divine grace, no matter how it is done. When we perform every duty detachedly with a sense of NK, the work itself becomes a worship of the divine. This is enough to invoke HIS grace; there is no need to separately worship the divine through complicated rituals. This saves us from pursuing GOD separately, through our work itself we can do that.

## How to gain spiritual knowledge?

For gaining spiritual knowledge one should have a clean mind. The mind is cleansed through yoga, which has 8 limbs. They are Yama (observances), Niyama (disciplines), asana (postures), pranayama (breath control), Pratyahara (control of senses), Dharana (concentration), dhyana (meditation) and Samadhi (absorption).

One has to practice yoga regularly in his day-to-day life to gain control of his sensory organs and slowly turn them internal. Untamed sensory organs are always turned external, which is a big problem because they always tend to get attracted towards the material objects.

While doing yoga, one should also gain the knowledge about the divine through various scriptures either by reading OR listening to lectures. However, one important thing he has to do is, constantly ask questions and seek answers within. The divine will answer them through "intuitional flash" and the answers come from within. Another important thing to practice is "observance". A GOD seeker should develop the habit of observing OR keenly watching everything happening around him, without any prejudice. Observe how things change in nature and that's when he will understand the power of the unknown, which is doing everything in the Universe.

So, with all these information, one can deduce that the purpose of life is to keep evolving from an imperfect to a perfect state. Make sincere attempts to acquire spiritual knowledge, so that one day, with the blessings of the divine, "GOD realization" happens.

Before I conclude this book, I want the readers to know about the concepts called and "Intuitional flash" and "Intellectual flash" which are related to our heart and brain. Knowing these flashes and putting them to use is very important for achieving material and spiritual excellence in life.

# Intellectual and intuitional flashes

**Introduction to Observation and Contemplation**

The philosophers always emphasized that one should learn the art of "observation and contemplation (O&C)", for making strides in the material and spiritual world. One is said to be leading a fulfilling life when he balances materialism with spiritualism together to make life worth living.

**What is Observation?**

Observation is very important for shaping up the human personality. However, we hardly do any observation. Let us dig a bit deeper to understand it.

There is an adage, "Man sees many things in his day-to-day life but hardly observes anything". Observing is also seeing but with full attention. However, we hardly do it because we either don't spare time OR don't have interest OR both.

**Why we rarely observe things?**

We lost our inquisitiveness that we once had when we were growing up as children. The children till 10 years of age generally have the curiosity to observe everything happening around them with "awe" but they lose it as and when they grow. However, this has repercussions on us, as we miss out on many things, life offers to us. Man cannot progress in life either spiritually OR materially OR both if he doesn't master the art of observation.

Let us understand what exactly is observation through an example below:

For example - We go to a supermarket to buy groceries and there we get to see many customers but we hardly observe them. That means, we hardly observe the customers as to what kind of clothes are they wearing? – Jeans & T-shirt OR traditional wear.

Do they generally buy more during the weekend OR at the beginning of the week OR midweek, so on and so forth. This is called an observation and it is of immense help to anyone who is into marketing/ sales. Having an eye for minute things is essential for man's progress in life because these small things always hide the big secrets of life.

Every event happening in our life leaves behind a trail of lessons – Good OR Bad. It is in our discretion whether to learn from it OR not. When we observe our own life and the events we came across, we learn lessons from them. Once the lessons learned, we don't tend to commit the same mistakes again and by this, we make progress in life.

Suppose we don't observe and learn from our life, we remain stagnated, committing the same mistakes again and again. Since we don't make progress in life, we get anxiety and suffer from depression.

In contrast, when we observe ourselves on a daily basis, we will understand us correctly. We will know what and what not to eat and how much to eat. This observation helps us eat right. We know when we lose temper and what is the trigger for our anger. This teaches us as to what we should do to not get angry. Every disease for example diabetes, blood pressure, anxiety, sleeplessness, etc. won't come all of a sudden. They start in a small way and take years to reach maturity. They would be sending signals about their arrival, but we tend to ignore them till they hit us hard on the face. These diseases could have been cured had they been noticed at the beginning itself. Any disease can be treated through medication at the beginning itself.

## The pitfalls of not cultivating the art of observation

There are many pitfalls in not having the habit of observing things in life.

- Diseases are not detected at the early stage

    We didn't observe ourselves in the first place and hence we never notice the existence of these diseases, so we ignore the subtle signals sent by them. Had we known, we would have taken corrective measures at the right time.

Like this, we will begin to know a lot about ourselves through self-observation and thanks to it, we will be able to lead a happy life.

- **Relationship suffers if not taken care in the early stage itself**

    Our societies are resting on the foundation of peace. If there is no peace in the society, man starts fighting and will be at each others' throat in the act of fury. If there is no peace, the societies will crumble and implode. Many societies perished earlier due to this and we have studied it in the history books. So, societal peace is very important for any society to exist. However, the peace rests on relationships, let us see how.

    If every individual develops the art of observing his neighbours and stops doing things which irk his neighbours, he will develop a good relationship with them. Likewise, if he has good relations at his workplace with clients, colleagues, superiors, subordinates, then he will prosper there. He can do that by applying the same formula of observation. By observing them carefully, he won't do anything which annoys them. Rather he does everything which attracts their appreciation. So, relationship blossoms.

Organisations which are built on strong relationships tend to perform better, as employees can understand each other well and are ever-ready to help. So, the life of individual employees will be at peace and graceful.

In case, we tend to skip observing, our relations with others get strained. As a result, we face huge losses and life can get that much painful to us. Like this, there are many more benefits of observation.

## What is contemplation?

O&C are the 2 faces of the same coin; one cannot exist without the other. Also, one can only contemplate what has been observed. Contemplation is also called "deep thinking", which is a hallmark for spiritual awakening. This is true of the material progress in life, as deep thinking results in either Intuitional OR Intellectual flash

- **Deep thinking is a part of contemplation**

    All great explorations, inventions & innovations, scientific & philosophical breakthroughs of the world have come out of deepest thinking and serious questioning by those people who didn't accept the status quo. Mysteries of the Universe have been unraveled this way. Similarly, one can get answers for anything one desires through deep contemplation. It could be a businessman finding ways to attract more customers, a scientist trying to crack a scientific puzzle, a father trying to resolve the family crisis and the like. Let's understand it briefly.

Example

Let's consider a businessman who is planning to invest in the expansion of his business, which will cost him substantially. He certainly will be perturbed as he may not be 100% sure if he is doing the right thing. Unable to crack this puzzle, he would consult his friends or experts but they too may give wrong suggestions on what he has to do. We have seen many incidences in the past where such suggestions have turned damp squib. Instead, if the businessman had done deep self-inquiry with the burning desire to know the answer, the divine itself would have answered through intuitional flash.

Since Intuitional flash (IF) is divine, it is holistic (all-encompassing) in nature. Hence it is more likely to be the right answer for the query. IF is much deeper and subtler than our thoughts and feeble in nature, hence not audible to us. So, when the mind is loaded with thoughts and emotions, it can't grasp IF. The mind can only catch IF when it is calm, with few or no thoughts in it, like when we are about to fall into sleep or relaxing while watching a movie or spending a good time with the family, so on and so forth. IF always comes as a feeling to us, not in sentences of any language that we use to communicate. Once the mind grasps the IF, it uses the intellect to decipher and understand it threadbare.

## Intellectual VS intuitional flash

Unlike IF, intellectual flash is much grosser and audible and in the face to us. It comes out through the process of logical reasoning as an end result of our analysis. Suppose if the businessman does a logical analysis to find out if his investment will be a success, what comes out of such analysis is an Intellectual flash. This is because; he uses his intellectual faculty for logical reasoning. However, there is one problem with this approach. Human intellect is limited in potential, as it can't perceive the truth in entirety. Hence, it ends up throwing the truth in bits and pieces OR wrong answer altogether and this becomes a bottleneck in itself. So, the logical reasoning with limitations may not be the appropriate way to grasp the truth. Intuitional flash is the right choice.

## How to get IF?

IF needs a lot of O&C and patience. One needs to stay calm to get the IF in the form of feelings. Some may get visions during meditation OR in the dream but the divine will surely answer the question, which is always the truth and hence dependable.

History records at least 2 cases of scientists using Intuitional Flash for scientific discoveries. Let's look into them briefly

## Past examples of Intuitions

### Archimedes

Archimedes (287 BC ~ 212 BC), an Italian mathematician and inventor, was ordered by his king to determine if the goldsmith had mixed any other metal other than gold, in making the royal crown. Archimedes worked intensely for days in his laboratory to devise ways to determine the volume of the crown with limited or no success. However, once when he was bathing at home at leisure, he saw water spillage from the water tub, when he got into it. Alas, he got the answer. He found out the way to determine the volume of an object. It came as an intuitional flash to him. He got over-excited and ran to the palace screaming "Eureka" without even wearing his clothes and the rest was the history.

## Sir Isaac Newton

Isaac Newton (1642 AD ~ 1727 AD), an English mathematician, physicist, and astronomer, seriously deliberating on natural forces of the earth was unable to crack it while working in his lab for days. Once an apple fell on his head while resting under an apple tree in his orchard. What his sleepless nights and hard work couldn't give, the sighting of an apple naturally falling down on his head from the tree, gave him the answer through Intuitional flash. He called the pulling force of the earth as "gravitation" and since then, he is known more for his work on gravitational science, than the other works he did during his lifetime and the rest is history.

Intuition won't work if the questions asked are too general, like "How will my life be, 5 years from now?" "How will my health be when I am 70 years old?", etc. For bringing harmony in life, one should develop the art of developing Intuition through which the divine guides him as to what he should do when he is at the crossroads.

## Knowledge and bliss are within us

Every Aatma has 4 kinds of bodies and they are one inside the other.

(1) Outer gross body (Saadhana Shareera in Sanskrit)

(2) Middle body (Sookshma Shareera in Sanskrit)

(3) Inner body (Linga Shareera in Sanskrit)

(4) Innermost body (JnanaAnanda Shareera in Sanskrit)

The outer body is the grossest and the innermost body is the subtlest.

For example, a suit worn by an individual can be imagined as the outer gross body – Saadhana Shareera. The shirt inside and the trouser below can be imagined to be the middle body – Sookshma Shareera. The inner-wear like brief and vests can be conceived to be the inner body – Linga Shareera and the real body of that individual is the innermost body – JnanaAnanda Shareera (JAS).

The outer body is the grossest body of all and we have that body for experiencing the past Karmic impressions and to perform Karmas, which keeps the flame of our future births burning. When we die, our Aatma departs by shedding the gross body and we continue roaming in that state until we are born again either as humans, animals, birds, reptiles, etc.

When there is the dissolution of the earth at the end of Chaturmukha Brahma Kalpa, which is Chaturmukha Brahma's one day (12 hours), Aatma loses Sookshma Shareera and it stays in the Linga Shareera till the beginning of the creation of the earth.

When the Aatmas complete their Saadhana by burning away all Karmic impurities through spiritual activities, they remain in the subtle world called "Sathya Lokha" – the world of truth. It is here, Chaturmukha Brahma (CB) resides with his eternal wife Bharathi.

The Aatmas in the Sathya Lokha will have permanently lost their first two bodies - the outer and middle ones and are left with only the inner body - Linga Shareera. At the end of Brahma Para Kaala, 100 years of CB, the Universal dissolution happens and the Aatmas (Sathvik ones) lose their Linga Shareera and enter the kingdom of GOD called Vaikunta to live there forever in a blissful state.

The body inside the Linga Shareera is the natural body of any Aatma, which is made up of pure Knowledge (material and spiritual) and Ananda (true bliss). It is only the right knowledge that brings the permanent bliss to the Aatma. However the Tamasik Aatmas do not have JAS, instead, they have Ajnana – loosely translated as wrong knowledge in Sanskrit and misery. Tamasik Aatmas have Ajnana Shareera (AS) and hence they suffer from misery unto eternity. This is because the wrong knowledge always leads to misery. On the contrary, Rajasik Aatmas (RA) have mixed knowledge – right as well as wrong. As a consequence of that, they (RA) experience bliss and grief alternatively, but they are short-lived.

## **What is bliss?**

To understand the meaning of bliss, let's consider our sleep. When we have good sleep overnight, we feel well rested and joyful as a result of it. It is to be noted that the joy comes from the bliss present inside our JAS. In fact, the outer reflection of our inner bliss makes us feel fresh and joyful after a good night's sleep and that's the truth.

In Vaikuntha, the Sathvik Aatmas live in JAS enjoying bliss until eternity. However, the depth and breadth of their bliss depend on the Kaksha in which they reside. Higher the Kaksha more is the knowledge and bliss.

So, our knowledge and happiness are always within. The knowledge comes out through intuitional flashes that too while doing unrelated work. It is also called as sudden revelation of the truth from within. The way in which the truth got revealed to Archimedes and Newton through intuitional flash supports the above statement.

When it comes to bliss, it always overflows from the inside out. for one to be happy and joyful in life and it supports the adage "When one is happy with oneself, he can be happy with others". So, in order to be good with others, we have to be good with us first. To be good with us, we have to be happy with ourselves.

Vedanta refers a Sathvik Aatma as "Sat-chit-Anand", loosely translated as an entity whose nature is knowledge induced bliss, which is permanent - forever.

# Conclusion

After reading the book, one question that arises in the mind of the readers is the following

Has the author of this book mastered Detached Attachment (DA)? – Understanding and mastering the concept of DA takes several lives if we start today. Therefore, one has to be in the GOD conscious state to get the sense of DA.

When we sink deep into the GOD conscious state, we will realize the eternal truth that everything – name, fame, money, etc. is temporary in nature and will end one day. Likewise, life too is temporary and we don't know when we will lose it. After this realization, we slowly lose interest or enthusiasm in all of these. Suddenly everything appears superficial and pales in comparison with the truth, we have to leave everything behind one day. That's when DA sets in automatically. The metamorphosis from this state is the state of "Sthitha Prajna" (SP), about which Lord Krishna speaking eloquently in the Bhagavad Geeta.

Everyone gets this feeling for sure, if not in this life, maybe in the future human lives. It all depends on where we are in the evolutionary path towards divinity. The trigger that pushes us to embrace DA is in the hands of GOD. When our time comes, the trigger happens automatically through the divine grace.

Nevertheless, to be in GOD conscious state continuously, we have to see GOD in everything we do and whomever we interact with on a daily basis, which is the most difficult nut to crack for an uninitiated mind.

The irony is that even with a lot of effort, one may learn to be in that state-of-mind only for a few moments. So, to lead one's whole life in the GOD conscious state, all he needs is wholehearted efforts and the divine grace. We have seen in the earlier chapters that the divine grace happens only at the appropriate moment and until then, one has to wait with steely patience.

The concept of DA and the transformation of an individual into 'Sthitha Prajna' is as much applicable to me as it is to anyone else. With GOD's grace, I have understood this eternal truth of DA and started adapting it in my life, little by little. Even with such a low adaptation, I am already experiencing inner joy. I feel much lighter from inside and life appears to be colourful to me when I see everything around me as a divine reflection. Thanks to the divine grace, I feel happy for whatever and whoever I am today.

Though I have just scratched the surface of DA, the return in the form of bliss I am enjoying is amazing. Now, imagine what will happen if I sink deep into DA? – Unexplainable bliss and I can say, spiritual ecstasy.  Being in the state of DA means being in communion with GOD. The Holy Scriptures describe the divine as 'infinitely blissful', 'infinitely knowledgeable', 'infinitely potent' and 'an all-pervading' entity with unparalleled humility. So being in communion with GOD means being in the divine consciousness and that means being blissful throughout.

With this, I end my book by thanking GOD for making me write it and using me to help the seekers of the divine to find HIM. I am also deeply indebted to GOD for choosing me to do HIS work of showing the path towards the divine for all its seekers.

Sri Krishnarpanamastu – I dedicate my Karma of writing this book to my beloved Lord Krishna and Sri Anjaneya (the incarnation of Sri Mukhya Prana - MP).

www.ingramcontent.com/pod-product-compliance
Lightning Source LLC
Chambersburg PA
CBHW032126160426
43197CB00008B/529